A Musician Talks

2. MUSICAL TEXTURES

A Musician Talks

2. MUSICAL TEXTURES

By

Donald Francis Tovey

GEOFFREY CUMBERLEGE
OXFORD UNIVERSITY PRESS
LONDON

OXFORD UNIVERSITY PRESS
AMEN HOUSE, E.C. 4
London Edinburgh Glasgow New York
Toronto Melbourne Cape Town Bombay
Calcutta Madras
GEOFFREY CUMBERLEGE
PUBLISHER TO THE UNIVERSITY

First published 1941
Second Impression 1942
Third Impression 1946

PRINTED IN GREAT BRITAIN

EDITOR'S NOTE

DONALD FRANCIS TOVEY was invited in 1936 by the University of Glasgow to deliver the Cramb Lectures, and in 1938 by the University of Liverpool to deliver the Alsop Lectures. University Lectures, daily or occasional, provided a medium in which Tovey felt comfortable, and these courses gave him an equal pleasure and incentive to express his ideas.

In prose-writing Tovey worked at his best with the printer's devil at his elbow. Not one of his now famous programme analyses had its origin save in a performance, not even from the days of the Meiningen Orchestra. He projected a number of books and editions. Yet of his published works only one, as far as I know, was the result of ignition without the tinder of performance—and that one was not entirely the result of spontaneous combustion. I refer to the *Companion to the Art of Fugue*. Even the cadenzas to classical concertos and the redistribution of the Hadyn trios could trace a lineage from actual concerts, and the *Companion* would never have been written had not Tovey delighted in playing the last Fugue of *Die Kunst der Fuge* with his own superlative ending.

For the appearance of these two volumes, issued under the name of *A Musician Talks*, I am partly responsible. To an extent Tovey needed his books to be made for him. One of the projects mentioned above was planned to fill a big frame. It was a series of text-books on music, to comprehend his own system of musical education. Their subjects were to be Counterpoint, Thorough-Bass, Form, and Orchestration. Not a word of them was ever written down. The scheme, however, simmered in his brain, and was after some years reduced to two composite books by his own wish. Still pen was not put to paper. Then came the call of the lectures, and at last Tovey, having accepted the invitations, was obliged to produce the matter in prose.

He dictated the lectures to his secretary and allowed the duplicate of the typescript to go to the printer and to be set up in type. But only those who were present at the delivery of the lectures can by comparison with this text have a real sense of how Tovey illuminated his words with the magic of his pianoforte playing. That a large part of the lectures was occupied by music is obvious: not only were there many long passages from the classical composers, but there were long improvisations in one style or another (cf. p. 27 of 'Musical Textures', where the lecturer showed how Klengel might have treated a given fugue subject).

On receiving his proofs Tovey was a little doubtful what to do about musical examples, as he was about the obvious overlapping of the two books in certain arguments and illustrations. To quote at anything like the length required would have turned a book into an album of music with annotations. But it was soon agreed that minor adjustments would avoid long citation. The overlapping I made light of, and Tovey also agreed to the issue of the books under the informal title they now bear. All was ready, but he was no diligent proof-reader, and he never corrected the proofs himself.

On his death, Lady Tovey kindly gave her consent to the publication of the books as they now stand. Also with her consent I invited Dr. Ernest Walker to contribute a Preface and give the proofs a final approval. The text exactly follows Tovey's words except for the main title, and except that certain small circumlocutions have been necessary, as I have explained above, to avoid musical examples, and certain corrections where the prose style betrayed dictation and lack of later revision. But I can testify that they are less in number than Tovey himself would probably have made.

For one admirer, at least, repetitions are but a slight disadvantage against the enormous advantage of the possession of two more of Tovey's writings.

HUBERT J. FOSS

November 1940.

PREFACE

DONALD FRANCIS TOVEY was born at Eton on 17 July 1875 and died at Edinburgh on 10 July 1940. My own acquaintance dates from October 1894, when he came up to Balliol as the first holder of the Lewis Nettleship Musical Scholarship: an undergraduate whose age was the only ordinary thing about him. With a winning personality keenly appreciative of the humorous, and abundant non-musical interests, he dropped easily into normal college life; but he had never been to a school of any kind, and had from early childhood been privately trained for the musical profession. There were other musically minded undergraduates in Oxford, but Tovey was very obviously in a class altogether by himself; not only was he an outstanding pianist, but the Bach-Gesellschaft scores were his regular bedside literature, and he had written full-dress symphonies—I still recall the opening page of one in E minor, and its author's innocent pleasure in the subtly artistic snag of the reiterated wind chords which, until the entry of the violins, suggested that the key was F major. A finely equipped musician in practice and in theory, the youth was father to the man. Tovey was a three-fold artist: in performance, in creation, in knowledge.

It was as a notably artistic pianist, in chamber music as well as in solo work, that Tovey was first generally known to the public: and throughout his life pianism, including problems of technique as well as of interpretation, remained a prominent though gradually a less absorbing interest. Among my own memories perhaps the most vivid are those of performances of the late Beethoven Sonatas, particularly op. 101 and op. 111: these were, very masterfully, the real thing. He was very versatile: Scriabin and Brucken-Fock and Hindemith had their turns as well as the classics. Line-drawing was nearer to his heart than niceties of colour; but anyhow it was always playing in the big manner, absolutely faithful and with finely modelled phrasing and a rhythm that could bend but never break. In his conducting, also, I always felt the same sure judgement of tempo; though he seemed less at home with London orchestras than with his more personally familiar Edinburgh folk.

Notwithstanding that he could complete Bach's *Kunst der Fuge* with dazzling certainty of style and technique, and write concerto-cadenzas that Beethoven and Brahms would have been glad to father, Tovey had as a composer a definite style of his own; and it changed little in essentials throughout his published work, from the op. 1 B minor Pianoforte Trio (dedicated to Parry as 'the first work of a grateful pupil') down to the end. In his earlier and more leisured life he was prolific; but after, in 1914, he had accepted the Reid Professorship of Music in the University of Edinburgh, and added to his other activities those of the busy and inspiring teacher and orchestral trainer, his output slackened a great deal. From time to time he showed me things that have, so far as I know, remained fragments; in these twenty-five years he produced for publication only two works, the choral setting of the Northumbrian 'Lyke-Wake Dirge', a miniature but none the less outstanding masterpiece full of a strange sombre beauty, and the spacious Violoncello Concerto, the finely massive first movement of which best, perhaps, represents his instrumental achievements. Otherwise I would direct special attention to the great closing scene of the opera *The Bride of Dionysus* (pre-1914, though not performed until later), the Variations for string quartet often played by the Busch Ensemble, the E minor Quartet for pianoforte and strings, the D major Pianoforte Trio (which I have heard its composer mention as if it were a rather favourite child), or, in lighter vein, the 'Balliol Dances' for pianoforte duet—the first five dating from undergraduate days, the remainder from considerably later. To the neophyte, these duets are the best of initiations into Tovey's compositions: we may feel the hand of Brahms in No. 5, but it is only a passing touch, and the transition from the penultimate to the last of the Dances is one of the most personal, and one of the most beautiful, things Tovey ever wrote. Though as a rule very quick in his literary work, he was a slow composer; and he suffered, possibly to his detriment, from a certain inability to leave a work alone when completed and performed, or even, in the case of the opera, when published. He could not, so to speak, refrain from fingering his creativeness. None the less, the creativeness is there.

It is, however, as a writer about rather than of music that Tovey has, at any rate up to the present, enjoyed the widest fame. He had read and remembered in detail and, what is more, methodically assimilated into his personal scheme of aesthetics, every page of live music from Byrd and Lassus and Palestrina to the end of the nineteenth century, with a great and varied mass of twentieth-century music in addition. The live music, I say; he was not the kind of scholar who is interested in a fact simply as a fact, and about dead music he did not worry. But he was not pedantically exclusive; some second-rank composers such as Méhul he had studied with minuteness, and he knew all that need be known about even third-rate folk. Unlike his Edinburgh predecessor and intimate friend, Frederick Niecks, he was not interested in composers' biographies: he knew Beethoven's works backwards, but cared nothing for his life—and less than nothing for attempts to correlate his music with the French Revolution. Definite artistic achievement of some kind was what mainly attracted him. He did not pay any very special attention to even creditable composers who, in his judgement, were merely pioneers or gap-bridgers: though his active dislikes were few—Saint-Saëns ('slick classicism' and 'thin, mundane lucidity') and, to a less extent, Liszt. Even then, he was catholic-minded enough to perform the Symphonic Poems of the former ('they are so damned clever'): and he was fond of Liszt's 'Orpheus', while often playing his transcriptions of Beethoven's Symphonies with enthusiastically admiring running comments.

Tovey was a brilliant talker: unfortunately he lacked a Boswell. But he often wrote in the same way that he talked; and we have from his pen six volumes of analytical essays, many elaborate articles in the *Encyclopedia Britannica*, the long essays on Brahms and Haydn in Cobbett's *Cyclopedic Survey of Chamber Music*, annotated editions of Bach and Beethoven, pamphlets, and many sporadic articles in journals and composite books, with various lectures —the Edinburgh inaugural, the Deneke and Romanes lectures at Oxford, the Hertz British Academy Lecture, and the Alsop and Cramb lectures first printed in these volumes. It is by these many hundreds of pages that he has achieved a world reputation; and, indeed, there is nothing like it all in English nor, so far as I know, in any other language. Perhaps we see the quintessence of his thought most completely in the Philip Maurice Deneke lecture on 'Musical Form and Matter', delivered at Lady Margaret Hall, Oxford, in June 1934: the germ from which the Cramb lectures in the present volumes have developed.

A great man must have his diversions; and, as all his acquaintances remember, Tovey had, all through his life, the keenest of appetites for wit, humour, and frank nonsense. The poetry of Edward Lear, Lewis Carroll, Hilaire Belloc, he knew by heart, set to brilliantly suitable music (unfortunately never written down), and sang *con amore*, along with advertisements, extracts from *Punch*, and so on *ad infinitum*; and in later life he added the *Galgenlieder* of Christian Morgenstern to his repertoire, though, I think, only for non-musical recitation. And, in one way or another, the same trait peeps out—or perhaps jumps out—in many a page of his critical writings: the index to his volumes of analytical essays, the last thing that he personally passed for press, contains entries that are nothing less than impish. A great man's diversions may often, to merely casual eyes, loom larger than they really are. With Tovey, anyhow, no one would have wished them otherwise. But as diversions they are a remembrance that will pass: it is the greatness that remains.

ERNEST WALKER

These lectures were delivered at the University of Liverpool under the James Alsop Foundation in April and May 1938.

Much of the Preface has already appeared in the pages of *The Monthly Musical Record*, and thanks are due to the Editor for kindly allowing this reprint.

CONTENTS

MUSICAL TEXTURES

MY general purpose in these lectures is to demon-strate that the art-forms of music when they attain their maturity are natural means of expression. Musical criticism has not accomplished its task until it has determined how far the form of the music is inherent in the matter. Nothing is easier than to classify musical art-forms and set up their criteria as if they were ideals that existed before the music was made for them. And no one can deny that a vast amount of substantially correct knowledge can be accumulated with the help of such classifications; yet there comes a point, sooner than we are ready to believe, where this kind of knowledge misleads. It is sure to mis-lead, for it is statistical knowledge, which in the last resort confesses that it does not and must not con-sider individual cases. Now, the very first thing that we need to grasp about a work of art is that each work of art is an individual case. Practically we are com-pelled to profit by the resemblances between a vast number of works of art. It is very doubtful whether we could fix our attention on any work of art unless a majority of its elements were familiar to us. It is only by that majority that we could notice the strangeness of the rest. On the other hand, where we can see no strangeness we can feel no interest. All that is new must be true, but it depends on our own experience how far anything is new. Now, it is a commonplace of enthusiasm to say that a great work of art is always new and never becomes stale. Like

most pious opinions, this puts a useless and dangerous strain upon faith. Even the most spiritual appe-
tite needs to be treated with reverent care; and much
of the world's worst criticism indicates a spiritual
indigestion which can result only from follies which
common sense would deem subhuman.

Such follies are often forced upon musical journal-
ists by their profession; but the *locus classicus* for the
promotion of musical indigestion was the quixotic
experiment of Hans von Bülow, who, under the
excuse that opportunities for hearing the work were
rare, gave a single concert consisting of two performances of Beethoven's Ninth Symphony. It is difficult
to conceive a worse way of trying to attain familiarity
with a great work of art, at all events if the work exists
in time rather than in space. Distributed over two
successive days, the experiment would have its value;
but except for a person on whom one performance
of the Ninth Symphony made no impression whatever, it would be difficult to conceive a more futile
effect than that of the opening of the symphony while
the end was still in one's immediate memory.

We must protect ourselves from all diseases of
criticism that can be traced to such unnatural acci-
dents; and we must view with caution all pious
opinions that make us over-confident in our musical
digestions. For example, it is often said in praise of
some simple touchstone of musical values that it still
remains beautiful after being heard hundreds of times
at a competition festival, whereas some popular suc-
cess of the day becomes intolerable after the fourth
hearing. My own experience has been otherwise.
I have often found that the manner and matter of the

popular rubbish soon vanished from my attention, leaving my mind free to concentrate on the merits of the competitors, but that the many performances of the good music soon began to sound as if the composer was repeating himself and accumulating into his work all the faults of the competitors. I am not myself addicted to the chewing-gum habit, but I understand that the slogan of the most widely advertised variety is that 'The Flavour Lasts'. But we need not pursue the inquiry as to whether works of art are to be ruminated on or straightforwardly swallowed and digested. On the whole, my own habits in the matter are bovine, and I prefer not to be hustled.

It has been well said that music shows a condition of purity and self-completeness which all other arts strive to attain as far as they can. Schweitzer illustrates an important consequence of this in his dictum that in music, of all arts, perfection is a *sine qua non* without which it cannot survive. Music has, indeed, obviously no practical or political reason for existing, unless it be to hold up to the world a demonstration that beauty and self-sufficing coherence are things attainable and attained. I have no ambition to prove any such audacious proposition, but, like the undergraduate whose Euclid paper failed to satisfy the examiners, though I may fail to prove it I hope to make it appear highly probable, at least in individual cases; and, as I do not believe in Art with a capital A, but only in individual works of art, my hope is not a logical impossibility. Of course, you must grant me an incalculable number of postulates and axioms. I can speak only from and for a musical experience of Western civilization in the last five centuries. I have not time to prove the inherent necessity of the musical system that has grown up within those limits, any more than I have time to debate whether other systems, ancient and oriental, have achieved a similar coherence and self-sufficiency; but I must lay down, firmly and dogmatically, that the musical system that we have established is not an artificial game, as has been suggested by Cardinal Newman and other thinkers. I think that in the course of a fairly long lecture it would be possible to prove, for example, that a chess problem, though it has many of the qualities of a work of art, is definitely not a work of art. It is derived from a game which presupposes a large number of rules that must be laid down beforehand. We are told that Capablanca in his earliest childhood discovered the rules of chess from watching his father and uncle play, and that he even caught the latter poor, but perhaps unscrupulous, player in the act of moving a castle like a knight. Yet I cannot persuade myself that the child Capablanca's miraculous instinct could elevate the rules of chess to the status of natural phenomena. On the other hand, similar and perfectly authenticated stories of the infant Mozart are one and all stories of self-explanatory musical experience, in spite of the astounding mechanical and physical aptitudes that they display. The child remembered the pitch of a violin's tuning within an eighth of a tone: without ever having had a lesson on a violin, he scrambled through a part in a string quartet, achieving right notes in the right time by wild-cat fingerings with a hand which was in any case far too small for normal positions. His earliest compositions, at first

4

dictated at the age of four, but soon written by his own hand, show a steady progress by trial and error. And it is perhaps dangerously easy to use them as evidence for my fundamental proposition that the foundations of music lie deeper in nature than the rules of a game. The danger is obviously that we have no means of knowing how much trial and error has disappeared from the records: besides which, many things have been falsely attributed to Mozart at every period of his miraculous career. One thing is quite certain, and that is that the prodigiousness of Mozart's childhood has not been in the slightest degree exaggerated: the falsehoods are mere nonsensical anachronisms, as much less wonderful than the facts as a magic carpet in *The Arabian Nights* is less wonderful than the scientific imagination of Leonardo da Vinci.

The rules of a work of art are not the rules of a game. With a few exceptions, like patience and solitaire, games are contests between adversaries; and even the solitary games contend against chance or time or Colonel Bogey. In the work of art there is no adversary; for by the time the work has come into existence the difficulties have ceased. We are concerned only with what the work is when it is finished. How it came into being is another story, which may explain, but cannot excuse, defects in the result. Many false criteria arise from confusing the practical means of composition with the essential results. Some of the best practical methods are fantastically remote from any aesthetic connexion with the work produced. When an English-speaking doctor wishes to ascertain the state of your throat and lungs he finds it convenient to judge by certain resonances produced when the patient pronounces the syllables 'Ninety-nine'. But ninety-nine is not a magic number with therapeutic virtues. For the English doctor's purpose its convenience leaves him no qualms about allowing panel patients to believe in it as a magic formula. It is not quackery to use it, and it would be worse than pedantry to avoid it.

There are many such analogies between medical devices and the methods which give rise to art-forms; and neither in life nor in art is there either an assignable limit to the elaboration of merely external methods, nor a clear line between the practical mechanism and the aesthetic essence. So long as we realize that the distinction is often important, we had better not be over-scrupulous about it where it is subtle. The object of discipline is freedom. Discipline forms habits which exemplify the principle of safety first, while at the same time we accumulate the skill and the knowledge which sets us free from slavery to those habits. Beethoven said that he learnt rules in order that he might know how to break them. The disciplinarian shrewdly remarks that Beethoven learnt the rules before he broke them. It is beyond my scope, and beyond my capacity, to go either into the origins or into the metaphysical foundations of art-forms; but I intend to deal as fully as your time and patience permit with the practical facts as recorded in classical music, going below the surface only in as far as this initial *caveat* compels me to do so.

Let us begin where, as far as I am concerned, straightforward enjoyment of mature Western music begins. Far be it from me to deny that there is a vast field of aesthetic delight in much more ancient music, and in highly organized and elaborate oriental music which is totally unintelligible to the Western musician's aesthetic organization. My subject is quite large enough and quite difficult enough if I take it as beginning with what is called the Golden Age of Music, a period roughly framed by the sixteenth century and not quite closed by the death of Palestrina in 1594. At the present day our current musical culture is very inadequately grounded. A well-informed taste for sixteenth-century music is still regarded as a special kind of scholarship, and few of our greatest musicians have opportunity for regarding the music of the sixteenth century as more than a subject for specialists. The Roman Catholic choirmaster and the conductor or organizer of a madrigal society are the only musicians who can normally know as much about some twenty great masters of the sixteenth century as every self-respecting all-round musician knows of Bach, Beethoven, Mozart, Brahms, and Wagner. The culture of the all-round modern musician is, indeed, wide, but so long as it does not strike its roots into the sixteenth century it remains on a level with that of the man of taste who a century ago appreciated all that he had seen and read during his grand tour, and to whom the Venus de' Medici and the Apollo Belvedere were the supreme masterpieces of Greek art, in comparison with which the Elgin Marbles were chiefly remarkable for the thick necks of 'those quaint, archaic horses'.

Every kind of information is welcome that can fill up such lacunae in one's aesthetic sensibilities. The first and most urgent step is to become familiar with the works in question. So long as interest is roused

7

and familiarity hastened, it does not at first matter whether the information that effects this is relevant or correct. The actual theorists of the sixteenth century were in some ways in a better position to throw genuine light upon their contemporaries than any other theorists in musical history. It so happened that during the career of Palestrina the important line of progress in music was a progress in purity. The purists were the persons of far-sighted intellect; and, roughly speaking, we may say that it was the inaccurate artists who were dull. At no later period in musical history has the academic theory been so completely in harmony with the finest musical inspiration of contemporary composers. In later times academic orthodoxy seems fated either to choose the wrong models for its forms or to set up forms that have never existed except for the sole convenience of the teacher. Cherubini's scheme for a fugue has not the remotest resemblance to any fugue by Bach, and needs some casuistry in its application to his own models: the orthodox explanations of sonata form are quite incapable of distinguishing genuine sonata style from the most flatly decorative and lyrical works, and fail even in externals to fit the average procedure of any composer except Spohr.

The academic orthodoxies of the sixteenth century have other defects. The theory is right in spirit, but is encumbered with the results of an extremely inconvenient point of view. A modern master of popular scientific exposition—that is to say, an eminent man of science—has remarked that when the phenomena compel a scientific theory to become fantastically complex we may foresee that we are observing the phenomena from the wrong point of view: as, for instance, when the motions of the planets require a tangle of deferents and epicycles, so long as we try to explain them as seen from a fixed earth instead of from a central sun. The whole trouble of the official theory of sixteenth-century harmony lay in the fact that the theorists retained the point of view of purely melodic scales long after these scales had become inveterately harmonic, as well as melodic, phenomena. The composers suffered nothing by the confusion. Palestrina and Marenzio composed hundreds of masses, madrigals, and motets in self-contained harmonic systems which could accommodate each specimen as easily as the alphabet can accommodate an index. The names of the modes implied certain real harmonic characteristics, about as accurately as 'Mac' implies a Scotsman and 'By Pol, Tre, and Pen you may know the Cornishmen'.

Palestrina could give technical reasons for assigning his compositions to twelve distinct ecclesiastical modes; and he has, in fact, two appreciably different kinds of major mode and three of minor. His major modes are the Ionian, the Mixolydian, and the Lydian; but, with one solitary exception, in all the thirty-four volumes of his works his Lydian mode is a mere transposition of his Ionian, which exactly corresponds to our modern major mode. His Mixolydian is like a modern major key balanced ambiguously on what is either a top-heavy dominant or an undermining subdominant. As a whole, the *Missa Papae Marcelli* is Ionian; but certain individual sections of it would be Mixolydian if we regarded them as complete, and nobody would notice any difference in tonality if whole pages were transferred to the *Missa Assumpta est Maria*, which is Mixolydian throughout.

Palestrina's three types of minor mode are the Dorian, the Phrygian, and the Aeolian. The scale of the Aeolian mode is easily described as that from which our key of A minor is derived; but, as a matter of fact, the harmony of Palestrina's Aeolian compositions is remoter from our ideas than anything else in his music. His Phrygian music sounds like an A minor with a habit of closing on the dominant, so that the composition seems to end with a half close. It is almost a matter of chance whether Palestrina will not end such a composition with what we recognize as a full close. This, of course, sounds perfectly normal to our ideas of A minor; but it does not change Palestrina's view of the Phrygian mode, or produce any approximation to his characteristic Aeolian harmonies. His Hypodorian music will pass for a quaintly coloured D minor, and his transposed Dorian for a similarly coloured G minor. In thus naming these keys I refer to the pitch of the notes as written by the composer. In practice the pitch was set by the choirmaster's pitch-pipe and determined by the convenience of the voices. Whatever fixed pitch might be settled for all music, some modes would lie too high for the voices and some too low. For Palestrina there was only one means of transposition available in writing, and that was effected by a key-signature of one flat, which either raised the whole scale by a fourth or lowered it by a fifth. With a fixed pitch such a wide transposition would merely shift the misfits to other modes. Our sixteenth-century masters early developed a sense of tonality much more like that of the eighteenth century; and they often employed a double transposition by means of two flats. In other respects also their harmonic range was the widest that the sixteenth century can show, both by retaining archaisms and by bold experiments. If we were to ask Weelkes the mode of his wonderful madrigal 'O care, thou wilt dispatch me', he would probably tell us that it was Phrygian. But for us it is simpler to regard its modulations as if they were by Schubert or Brahms at their highest flights of imagination. To explain them aesthetically as Phrygian is to search for the Scottish ancestors of a notorious Semitic moneylender trading under the name of Macgregor.

The modes were no shackles to the sixteenth-century composer. He had no scruple in overriding the official theory for the sake of any effect of harmonic colour that pleased him. If you ask a connoisseur of sixteenth-century music to quote a typical example of modal harmony, the chances are that he will give you the opening of Palestrina's *Stabat Mater*, and may perhaps volunteer the information that it is Dorian. But there is not a single characteristic of this wonderful phrase that is not Palestrina's individual stroke of genius. All that the Dorian mode has done to help in the matter is to leave him unvexed by the harmonic habits that would compel later composers to assert the key of D minor or any definite key. Some ninety years ago, when William Byrd's *Cantiones Sacrae* were published for the Musical Antiquarian Society by Mendelssohn's friend Horsley, that editor quoted the opening of Palestrina's *Stabat Mater* as 'a curious instance of the uncertainty relative to the scale prevalent in the time of the author'. To the sixteenth-century composer there was no uncertainty relative to the scale. There was a glorious tangle of dogmas, which fortunately gave him dozens of definite ortho-doxies to choose from and a clear consciousness and boldness when he preferred to be unorthodox. With the rise of instrumental and dramatic music in the seventeenth century came an unlimited freedom, the first effect of which was to paralyse composition rather than to emancipate it. The seventeenth cen-tury is a paradise for the kind of musician who is more interested in historic processes than in artistic re-sults. Nearly everything that happens in the music of the seventeenth century is interesting as the origin of something else; and by diligent research and discrimination it is possible to accumulate a large anthology of seventeenth-century masterpieces, each interesting and beautiful in itself, and each doubtless illustrative of some important historic tendency, but impossible to group into definite schools, or even, on internal evidence, to assign to definite dates. Present me with a perfect performance of Schütz's *Lamentatio Davidi*, with a first-rate singer, four trom-bones, and an organ, and ask me to judge by its purely musical values when it was written. I have no means of knowing that it was not written the day before yesterday by Holst or Vaughan Williams in a mood of inspiration which happened to exclude both the more modern and the more deliberately archaic fea-tures of their styles. Present me with almost any random short quotation from Purcell, and I would guess that this must be by some composer of the calibre of Bach or Handel, though evidently neither of those masters. From a short quotation, I could certainly not guess the lamentable fact that Purcell was almost always prevented from building a coherent work of art on a large scale. It is a fascinating occupation to roam through the music of the seventeenth century in search of beautiful and stimulating passages; but the connoisseur whose favourite period in music is the seventeenth century is farther from the truth than one who accepts the comparatively philistine judgement that between the death of Palestrina in 1594 and the birth of Bach and Handel in 1685 there are no great composers.

The general texture of an art—that is to say, the general power of fluent expression in its medium—becomes mature long before the external art-forms can attain anything beyond an obviously mechanical organization. In this respect the substance of the art stands to the theory of the art-forms much as the phenomena of nature stand to scientific theory. At first the recognizable art-forms are evidently external, *a priori*, and crude. For the artist their duty is to enable him to get on with his work without waiting for an inspiration which will never come until something has been begun. An ingenious theory has been propounded that in an age demonstrably before the art of writing the *Iliad* was preserved by being constructed in cantos of 300 lines, so that the rhapsodist could keep tally of his sections by counting the lines on a rosary. The practical value of such a scheme is obviously vital, and its difficulties are negligible to such a supreme master as the creator of a microscopically fine texture of Homeric verse; but it is not in itself an aesthetic quality. Certain Hebrew poets have found an aid to memory in arranging the lines of their poems in an alphabetical acrostic. This is a much more artificial scheme that must interfere much more constantly with the substance of what the poet has to say; but its effects, whether good or bad, vanish in translation, and we should never have suspected it in the Lamentations of Jeremiah if our Bibles had not preserved the letters of the Hebrew alphabet in the margin. Nor would anybody have attached much importance to them if Palestrina and his predecessors had not acted on the pious superstition that they were magic formulas and had not set them to elaborate polyphony, like illuminated initials, at the beginning of each section of their composition of the Lamentations.

Most of the history of sixteenth-century art-forms develops on these lines. The nearest analogy in nature is that of a saturated solution of some compound that can crystallize. Drop a thread or a wire into that solution and crystals will form around it. Bend your wire into any shape you please and your crystalline object will be ordered by that shape. Your wire or string may remain, buried or visible, as the sixteenth-century *canto fermo*, sacred or secular, may remain in long notes in the tenor part of a Mass by Josquin. The shape of the object round which the crystals form may make remarkably little difference to the result. Palestrina wrote one of his best Masses around a second soprano that sang the notes of the hexachord, *ut*, *re*, *mi*, *fa*, *sol*, *la*, up and down throughout the whole work. He also wrote one on an old French song, 'L'homme armé', which had for the last hundred years served as a sort of hobby-horse for all the athletics of fifteenth- and sixteenth-century counterpoint and rhythm. The popular academic theory holds that the music tended to be vitiated by the extravagant ingenuity of the contrapuntal athletics. This is not what really happened. The tendency of first-rate athletic displays of all kinds is to look easy, even when evidently dangerous. Awkwardness and ugliness do not result from contrapuntal ingenuity, and the ugly displays are *ipso facto* bad counterpoint. The trouble that arose, and to which the Council of Trent objected, was that the composers and singers tended to associate the threads of *canto fermo* with their original texts, with results which were confusing to the liturgy when the texts were edifying, and obviously scandalous when the texts were not. In any case, it is quite easy to contrive that the thread round which you form your crystals shall be dissolved or extracted; and in that central masterpiece of pure polyphony, the *Missa Papae Marcelli*, we reach the consummation of Palestrina's highest art in a work so contrived that every word of the liturgical text is heard, that the polyphony is of the highest order, and that there are no recurrent themes whatever, except the first of all, which might have come from anywhere, but which happens to be the first figure of the notorious 'L'homme armé'. I cannot help suspecting Palestrina of an amiable appeal to the Divinity to forgive him for an affectionate loyalty to paganism.

And so the texture of sixteenth-century music consists mainly of a kind of crystalline counterpoint, from which in the most mature examples the mechanical, or foreign, cause that precipitated the crystals has disappeared. There is only a difference of degree between the most elaborate counterpoint and the severest homophonic style, such as that of Palestrina's *Stabat Mater* and *Improperia*, and that of Tallis's *Responses*: music in which the voices deliver plain concords in homogeneous rhythm with no display of contrapuntal device whatever. In the severest music of this *stilo popolare* the voices are contrapuntal inasmuch as they preserve their independence. There is an Italian miniature full score of Rossini's *Guillaume Tell*, published in the 1860's, with a preface almost as delightful as the music. The adoring editor calls attention to a passage in which Rossini perpetrates one of his naughtiest sentimentalities by way of expressing the melancholy with which the Swiss regard the setting sun. Upon which the editor remarks that the great Palestrina, perhaps with the same intention as Rossini, has used a similar strange succession of chords at the beginning of his famous *Stabat Mater*. Perhaps the editor thought it pedantic to remark, though it seems incredible that he should not have known, that Palestrina's chords are in perfect counterpoint, whereas Rossini's anticipate the most disciplinarian modern anarchies by violently denying every grammatical principle of classical music.

The chief, and in the music of the sixteenth century the only, foundation of musical texture is the nature of the human voice, treated in chorus and on the basis that the choral harmony is woven of independent strands, each of which has its own melodic value. The enormous range of the monodic revolution at the turn of the century, and the chaos which it needed almost the whole seventeenth century to clear up,

represent essentially the discovery that instruments
are not voices. Instruments have their own characters
as well as an immense capacity to imitate and to transcend voices. Reciprocally, voices can learn to do
many things which would never have occurred to a
composer except at the suggestion of instruments.
Our musical culture will always be lacking in its
appreciation of what voices can do in their own right
until it has thoroughly grounded itself in the styles
of the Golden Age of Music; and until we have thus
grasped the central facts of pure vocal harmony there
will always be something lacking in our understanding of instruments. The foundations of musical
grammar will always remain based upon the principles of vocal harmony. These have been mastered
in classical counterpoint, whether as homophonic as
Tallis's *Responses* or as polyphonic as his most amaz-
ing canonic ingenuities. In relation to voices, instruments have two aspects. They can imitate voices,
sometimes so perfectly that I have succeeded in
getting an audience in the school-room of a Welsh
country parish to sing Bach's great E major Fugue
with me in four-part harmony after I had played it to
them three times. The keyboard of the pianoforte
and of the organ is expressly designed so that an
ordinary pair of hands can tackle most of the intervals
that are likely to occur in choral harmony. The organ
has a superhuman sustaining and breathing power.
The pianoforte has an evanescent tone, which does
not vanish so quickly that it cannot suggest considerable vocal powers. The pianoforte is also admirably
apt to display the opposite function of instruments,
the function of supporting and contrasting with

voices by thrumming and drumming. The harp is an attractively sensuous medium for supporting voices with masses of harmony that reverberate and can produce percussive rhythms; but when we ask it to sing by itself we cannot long remain amenable to its feeble power of suggesting sustained tone, and one of the funniest things I can ever remember to have heard was the performance by a famous harp-player of one of the most famous pieces of pianistic thunder, Rachmaninoff's Prelude in C sharp minor.

Of late years the treatment of most instruments has been appallingly vulgarized by precious and obvious theories as to their functions. An indecent X-ray examination of the interiors of pianofortes has revealed that the pianoforte-strings are set in vibration by the impact of hammers; and composers who ought to know better are nowadays conscientiously refraining from anything which displays the pianoforte in any other light than that of this mechanical fact. It is difficult to see much aesthetic depth in dogmas which insist on a mechanical detail to the total exclusion of the effect of the mechanism. The composer who devoted himself most exclusively and imaginatively to the pianoforte is Chopin, and though in his time the sustaining power of the instrument was far less than it is nowadays, no composer has more boldly relied on its power of suggestion. I had the privilege of knowing an authority who heard Chopin play, and who was himself the head of the firm of Broadwood's, the late A. J. Hipkins. If anybody knew that the pianoforte was, as Beethoven and his publishers in a few years of linguistic chauvinism called it, a *Hammerclavier*, it must have been Hipkins; but he always described its character as that of an instrument with an evanescent tone. The actual length of the tone is not so important as the smoothness of its evanescence. I should be very glad to meet a violinist who could control a diminuendo as perfectly as a good pianoforte can control the diminuendo of the longest note in Chopin's D flat Nocturne.

Let us then conclude by summarizing the general texture of music as essentially and centrally the texture of choral polyphony, with a background and framing of all that arises from the nature of instruments designed partly to imitate and transcend voices, and partly to support and contrast with them. The vocal aspect is typified by song, and the instrumental aspect by dance. The interactions between the two are infinitely numerous, and there is abundant room for truth and falsehood in them. One of the truest examples of a subtle interaction between the extremes of vocal and instrumental aesthetics is the first prelude of the *Wohltemperirtes Klavier*, the simplest and, if comparisons are possible, the most beautiful of Bach's arpeggio preludes. The very word 'arpeggio' is derived from the harp, because of the habit of that luscious instrument to deliver its dollops of harmony in successive notes rather than in hard, unbroken chords. Bach's first prelude thus displays almost the most primitive qualities of instrumental music. You might perhaps sink farther into pure instrumentality by writing for drums, but you will not get much music out of them; yet Bach's first prelude is also a perfect piece of five-part polyphony. His arpeggio formula would be equally capable of outlining Palestrina's *Stabat Mater*, and the ear would instantly resent its degeneration to the Alpine sunset of Rossini.

Of instrumental art-forms Bach's arpeggio preludes represent the simplest. At the other extreme we have the fugue, which consists essentially of the working out of a pregnant phrase by something equivalent to a chorus in a definite number of parts. The fugue is thus originally a choral art-form; and it may be worked out on a keyboard as vocally as that great classic of Bach which I made the Welsh schoolroom audience sing after three hearings, or its themes may range anywhere between such vocal types and the most outrageously instrumental propositions. The rules of fugue as an art-form have been drawn up mostly with regard to the sole convenience of teachers and with no regard whatever to the practice of classical composers, except, paradoxically enough, in certain vexatious minutiae about the relation between subject and answer. As the rules were drawn up by teachers to whom Bach was either unknown or an object of strong disapproval, this is perhaps not surprising. You *may* perhaps be surprised to find that I have otherwise no positive doctrine to offer in these lectures as to the fugue as an art-form. Fugue is an art-form only in the sense that verse is an art-form. Polyphonic compositions are written more or less in fugue. When such a composition is nothing but fugue it is convenient to call it a fugue, but nothing but confusion arises from trying to regard fugues as shapes. A tolerable analogy to the position of fugue as an artistic medium is the position of blank verse in English literature. It is utterly misleading to argue from the elaborate rules that have been laid down for vocal construction that a fugue has any kind of aesthetic resemblance to a sonnet. You need not therefore be surprised to find that all that I have to say about this ostensibly most learned and elaborate of art-forms will be dissolved in my next lecture, the subject of which will be Musical Rhetoric.

MUSICAL RHETORIC

ALL musical art-forms are remarkably easy to describe, both in general and in detail. This has its dangers, and my own conviction grows steadily, that for the teaching of composition the dangers outweigh the advantages. The imposing façade of the generalized formal outlines and definitions conceals the features of the individual work of art and produces in our minds a confusion like that of the Bellman in *The Hunting of the Snark*, who preferred the guidance of a map which was an absolute blank. 'Other maps', he said, 'are such shapes, with their islands and capes', which, no less than Mercator's poles and equators and other geometrical co-ordinates, he dismissed as 'merely conventional signs'. The Bellman's conclusion is no model of freedom of thought, either in navigation or art. Musical art-forms have often been incorrectly generalized, and the correct generalizations of one language have often been mistranslated into other languages. It is tiresome to reiterate this; and I prefer to use my own terminology and to describe the facts in the plainest English that I can achieve; but I cannot regard either the generalized art-forms or the features of individual works of art as merely conventional signs. And I recommend to all lovers of music a grave mistrust of all criticism that stresses the importance of convention—and, indeed, of all knowledge that could not ultimately be derived from the contents of each individual work without reference to other works. Let us by all means remember that life is short, and that we must therefore fore-shorten our experience of art to bring it within human compass; and let us accordingly use our knowledge of fugues and sonatas in general so that we may recognize of any individual composition that this is a fugue or this is a sonata, so that we may be satisfied where it behaves as we expect fugues and sonatas to behave, and surprised where it does not. But neither our satisfaction nor our surprise will be well grounded until we can find its ultimate explanation in the individual work without reference to any other work or to any statistical information. The generalities we must consider are more universal than music itself. The most fruitful and the least misleading term that I can find for my subject to-day is 'rhetoric'. You will not expect me to link up every step in my argument in strict accordance with my general *caveat* against generalizations. I might succeed in proceeding legitimately from one step to the next; but it would be equally legitimate for your more agile minds to withhold your attention. So I will jump at once into the most tangled of technicalities, and begin by demonstrating the purely rhetorical common sense of some of the minutiae of tonal fugue.

What is a fugue? A fugue is a composition written wholly in fugue—that is to say, in a texture woven by a definite number of voices, vocal or instrumental, who discuss on equal terms a definite theme. At all periods of classical music and modern music a composer is as much at liberty to break into fugue as a dramatist or novelist is at liberty to break into verse. A writer of serious prose will not inadvertently break into rhyme or into the rollicking rhythm

23

of the limerick; but critics will notice as a defect the tendency of sentimental prose to drift into blank verse, as Dickens drifts in his account of the death of Little Nell.

In its convenience and fluency, fugue-texture has a place in music not unlike that of blank verse in literature. The form of a scholastic fugue, as laid down by Cherubini, is a fiction devised for the sole convenience of the teacher. It is harmless as an exercise, but few things in musical education are more disastrous than the sheer mendacity that results from trying to reconcile the practice of great composers with it. The only part of the scholastic doctrine that is true and well observed is the most vexatiously technical of all: namely, the relation between subject and answer. Rightly understood, this illustrates many fine points in the nature of musical rhetoric. At the beginning of a fugue the normal situation is that a single voice propounds a subject—that is to say, a pregnant piece of melody not so complete as to come to a full stop, and not so fragmentary as to state nothing. This subject is promptly answered by another voice at a different pitch. The voices of a human chorus fall naturally into the classes of soprano, alto, tenor, and bass. Soprano and tenor are roughly an octave apart, alto and bass lie normally a fourth or a fifth below soprano and tenor. These pitch-relations are obviously reproducible by human hands on a keyboard and by groups of instruments. In a fugue there is obviously more variety if the answering part is a fourth or a fifth below the leader than if it is at the octave or unison. Now the question at once arises whether the alternation between subject and answer is an alternation between two keys, or an alternation between two positions of the same scale. Mozart's *Musikalischer Spass*, which has been solemnly described as a caricature of the convention of his day, is something much deeper and more amusing. It is a faithful study of the phenomena of ignorance, subtle enough in some points to deceive the editors of the band-parts, who have corrected some of its mistakes. Its Finale breaks, at the expected moment, into fugue as conceived by the unlearned. There is nothing wrong with the subject, nor with the answer, nor with the countersubjects, of which there are two; but this shows what happens when the answer is crassly conceived as in another key from the subject. There is a certain stiffness about the procedure, and we need not be surprised if the bucolic composer is tired of contrapuntal writing when the fourth voice enters. When the answer is an exact transcription of the subject it is called real, but even a real answer need not be harmonized flatly in its own key. To many subjects, such as this of Mozart's and about half of Bach's or any other composer's, only a real answer is possible, but you will seldom find a masterly composer effecting the transition without some glide in the harmony—if, indeed, the pitch of the answer establishes a new key at all.

But a large number of fugue subjects, perhaps a majority, need changes in the answer, and such modified answers are called tonal. The rules governing details of tonal answers are vexatious. They often, as in the cases I have just cited, will produce a real answer; and there are numerous cases where it is said to be difficult to find a correct answer. The recent very learned treatise on *La Fugue d'École* makes out an excellent and honest case for the admittedly fictitious scholastic fugue as a discipline, but in my opinion demolishes its case completely by gravely demonstrating that for a certain subject beginning with three adjacent notes the only correct answer is one of three identical notes, whether the fugue be scholastic or genuinely musical. The rules which make such a case difficult ought to be swept into limbo. Three identical notes are on no conceivable ruling an answer to a subject of three different notes. The case is like demanding a plain answer, 'Yes or No', to the question: 'Have you left off beating your wife?'

The rhetorical common sense of the rules that produce tonal answers becomes self-evident when we take typical instances. There are two main cross-sections of the scale, in one of which the tonic is the melodic centre, and in the other the dominant. Where either note is prominent it is answered by the other, and where in one position a melody has a fifth in which to move it will have only a fourth in the other position. The relation between these positions is described in terms of the ecclesiastical modes, as the relation between the authentic and plagal; but as a matter of history the tonal fugue did not take shape until the seventeenth century.

In the nineteenth century there appeared a very meritorious work by one Klengel, consisting of forty-eight canons and fugues in all the major and minor keys, as in Bach's *Wohltemperirtes Clavier*. The people who were deceived by it were on the whole wiser than those who saw through it at once. For it is possible to see so instantly through things as to see

26

nothing in things. The criticism that poor Klengel's work was all technical and had no poetic merit or musical imagination was quite unfair. Klengel had quite a pretty imagination and considerable invention. The form of a canon is so restricted that even with Bach it is hardly more suitable than an acrostic to be stretched beyond the dimensions of an epigram; yet Klengel's canons are free from the defect that ruins most of his fugues, because the exigencies of canon prevent him from indulging in his fatal habit of writing in four-bar periods and sitting down in full close at each fugue entry—defects which my counter-point master, James Higgs, would never have al-lowed to pass in my scholastic exercises.

Now here is the subject of one of Bach's most famous fugues:

It so happens that the rules of tonal fugue leave room for nothing but a real answer. We may speculate how Klengel would have created the ex-position: there would have been nothing wrong with it in sense or grammar, nothing less than one could reasonably expect from a good student. But we remember what Bach made of it.

We need no vague, pious opinion to stimulate our sense that this is good rhetoric. Still less do we need a technical explanation of its points—or, rather, the true technical explanation is precisely the rhetor-ical common sense of every detail. The normal harmo-nization of the answer would certainly be in the dominant rather than on the dominant, and Bach is compelled to be specially emphatic to contradict this. When the fourth voice enters, a dominant answer could hardly be again contradicted without exactly the same emphasis; and Bach is not ready to weaken his resolve to avoid the dominant key. Hence, he ignores precedent and gives us a new answer that visits the subdominant and is overlapped by the entry of the fifth voice. The overlap speeds up the rhythmic flow; and the harmony is diverted away from the tonic. All the voices are now present, so that, according to the technical terminology, the exposition is complete. Not so, however, the essentially musical section. As the harmony drifts, one of the lower voices gives the subject (or answer, whichever you prefer to call it) for the first time really in the key of the dominant, and brings us to the first full close, through which, however, the music continues to flow until two other entries bring us to a definite close in another key, E major.

Now from this point the fugue develops on a much larger scale and with much livelier rhythms, consisting essentially of an incessant whirl of three themes in combination. I will not deal with the rest of the fugue, but will point out that, if this C sharp minor Fugue were the only one in the world, its anomalous fourth entry would appear as a self-evident necessity, much more like an example of a rule than a breach of it.

In great fugue-writing the rules of rhetoric are very easily traced. According to the scholastic theory, stretto, or the piling up of close overlaps between subject and answer, is an obvious means of climax. Cherubini naïvely remarks that its effect is highly piquant; and he prescribes that the stretti should be contained in the last section of a fugue, and should be preceded by a pause on the dominant of the minor mode. Of this naïve scheme Bach shows no consciousness whatever. He does not arrange his stretti in order of closeness, he does not often reserve them for the end of a fugue, and if we were to accept the academic doctrine that every fugue subject ought to be capable of at least one good stretto we should have to exclude, not only two-thirds of Bach's free compositions, but, as far as the use of stretto is concerned, two-thirds of his last work, *Die Kunst der Fuge*, which he devoted expressly to the illustration of his own most abstract ideas of fugue structure.

Musical rhetoric can never depend upon the alleged difficulty or ingenuity of its mechanism. It depends very obviously upon such natural phenomena as the emotional effect of top notes in the human voice, and upon every means of spacing out events and varieties of rhythm. The means of musical rhetoric become greater in proportion to the length of time over which the composer appeals to our memory. Palestrina's setting of a Mass may fill as much as half an hour, and may use the material of a single motet or other source of themes recognizably throughout. But he does not rely upon our recognition, and the aesthetic time-limit of any of his real designs ranges from a normal three minutes to a rather exceptional ten.

The sixteenth-century composers' themes are fitted to the words that are sung; and it is by no means the case that in mature examples the words are repeated without limit and rational cause. In a polyphonic design they will be repeated until all the voices have had a share in them. The average motet may contain some four or five sentences; the last sentence may be expanded in a climax; and certain exclamations, such as 'Alleluia' and 'Amen', may be developed at length. Otherwise there will be little more repetition than is necessary to make the words understood at all when the polyphony is involved and the voices overlap. Moreover, the general policy is to deliver a whole sentence without interruption before breaking up its clauses. Palestrina has little opportunity for the transcendent rhetorical powers that result from music that builds itself into large symmetrical patterns. Sixteenth-century music is aesthetically equivalent to the decorating of a space, but not to structure on an architectural scale. The nature of larger musical structures will make the listener expect a much more cogent rhetoric than he will find in Palestrina. The balance of a perfect Palestrina motet is far more subtle than anything which we are called upon to analyse in later music. Its effects of climax, by expansion and crowding of rhythms and by well-placed high notes in the inner as well as in outer parts, are, though very intense, more analogous to the sounds than to the sense of poetry. The quiet opening of Bach's C sharp minor Fugue is a far more solid structure than anything within Palestrina's scope. On the other hand, it stimulates the attention and memory to trace lines of rise and fall over far longer time-intervals than any to which the sixteenth-century composer directs his attention. If you are un-accustomed to the principles of sixteenth-century music you will be ready to accuse Palestrina of a defective sense of climax, because you will expect a high note in one place to produce a corresponding one long after Palestrina has effected all that he meant by it and directed his mind elsewhere. This is as if you should fail to appreciate blank verse and incur Milton's good-natured toleration of the younger poet whom he allowed to tag his verses and turn *Paradise Lost* into heroic couplets. I have compared Bach's fugue-texture with that of blank verse, and I do not mean that to criticize Palestrina from the point of view of Bach is as bad as to turn the magnificent flow of the C sharp minor Fugue into the squareness and stiffness of Klengel. The heroic couplet cannot produce Milton's magnificent verse-paragraphs, but it is no crude or unresourceful means of expression.

I have now spoken of the musical treatment of words; but that vast subject does not include the aspects of musical rhetoric with which I intend to deal, though it is the occasion for several dangerous and plausible fallacies against which we must take timely warning. In recent times great composers have themselves been misled by facile doctrines about musical declamation which have seldom or never deceived the poets. The modern musician has a sense of musical accent which is enormously stronger than that of the poet, for it is far more akin to dance-rhythm than to speech-rhythm. Poets who are not musicians do not always recognize this difference, which, indeed, did not become important until the music of the eighteenth century was mature. With great composers such as Bach, Mozart, and Schubert, the genius for the declamation of words seems to be a function of their normal melodic power; so that they do not even attract the attention of the conscientious critic to their verbal accentuations, even though these are often recklessly defiant of the rules which critics try to lay down. The difficulties first arise with composers who have had leisure to deliberate about the problem. The tendency of these composers is to form an inadequate theory of verse-rhythm and a theory of musical accentuation violently stiffened by the convention of musical notation which divides the music by bar-strokes at equal intervals and regards these strokes as implying overwhelming muscular stress.

The fallacy ruins the reciting of verse before the words are set to music; and it misleads composers into the disciplinarian commonplaces of a characteristic musical anarchy. Before its victims were musicians, they recited all verse as if it were prose curiously disarranged for no discoverable reason. This disarranged prose is then sung to music which seems to avoid making melodic sense for no other reason than that a voice should never sing anything that would be intelligible on an instrument. This is, of course, in accordance with a kind of functionalism which has produced grotesque consequences in all the arts: the view that does not recognize that instruments are made for music, but insists that music is so made for instruments that no oboe should play what could be played by a clarinet or vice versa, and in the last resort that no gentleman should say what could be said by a lady and no lady should say what could be said by a gentleman.

Now, we shall never begin to understand musical rhetoric until we realize: first, that not only are the habits of verse widely different from those of prose, but that the habits of music are widely different from those of words; and secondly, that it lies in the very nature of art to reconcile such oppositions, and that nothing is more radically inartistic than to sacrifice one of the opposing principles wholly to the other. It is doubtful whether art begins to exist without a reconciling of opposite claims, not by compromise, but by actual indissoluble compounding. The composers who have begun to worry about declamation are in most cases precisely those in whom the declamation really goes wrong, sometimes according to their own theories, and generally because they are attending only to the prose-sense of the words. This is a subject for a whole course of lectures; but, unfortunately, to discuss what is relevant here would carry me too far away from the rhetoric of music by compelling me to give too much attention to the rhetoric of words. Time permits me here only to say that the most fundamental fallacy of the prose-declamatory view of song is the doctrine that a composer who sets many verses of a lyric poem to the same melody is doing a lazier and lower thing than the composer who sets the poem to music which corresponds with the sense line for line and word for note. No poet has fallen into such an error. The poet knows that a melody is a thing that can often shed more light upon words by not changing with them than by changing with them. Emotionally it can be as the weather and the scenery in relation to a group of human beings: nature and bird-song and sunshine in sympathy with our happiness, and the same sky as brass above us when disaster has befallen.

Wagner is supposed to have laid down the lines of musical declamation inexorably in Hans Sachs's criticism of poor Beckmesser in *Die Meistersinger*; but the details of his criticism show an argument which is remarkably the opposite of that which puts the words above the music. He corrects Beckmesser's first false accent by fitting Beckmesser's tune to a natural accent. But Beckmesser complains that the correction wipes out the rhyme, to which Hans Sachs asks: 'Then don't you care for the tune?' And, when in the third act the hero sings the prize-song of his dream and Sachs takes down the words at his dictation, Sachs's comment is that it is a nice tune for which to write poetry. Brahms, who thought deeply about musical declamation and considered the strophic song with an identical tune a far higher achievement than anything *durchcomponirt*, is often reckless about his accentuation, and not always defensibly; but he is often blamed for what an unprejudiced poetic ear would recognize as a much-needed revival of a sixteenth-century rhythmic elasticity. Such a song as 'Wie bist du, meine Königin', which is often supposed to be a model of bad declamation, is closely parallel to one of our Jacobean English masterpieces, Dowland's 'Awake, sweet love'; and Dowland expressed highly conscientious views about his declamation.

Apart from these subtleties of the nature of verse and of musical rhythm, we shall never begin to understand musical rhetoric until we realize that on a large scale music is as dependent upon actual repetition as architecture is dependent upon symmetry. Wagner is popularly supposed to have broken down all musical symmetry until his music became a flowing medium that could be spread over a drama as butter can be spread over bread. There is need for a treatise on the mature works of Wagner as pure musical compositions. In Wagner's later operas the time occupied by solid musical recapitulations is as great as that occupied by the recapitulations in classical symphonies. The lines and occasions for recapitulation are not symphonic, nor otherwise conventional. The singers often remain unconscious of them, because the words are not recapitulated and the new words require different vocal parts. If a defect can be imputed to Wagner's mature style, it is that the voice, which inevitably forces everything else into the background of our attention, is too often imposed upon the orchestra like something as extraneous to the design as writing would be to the surface of a picture. I confess that I have often wished that I could enjoy the composition of *Die Meistersinger* without attending to the singing, except where the voices are set free by the hypothesis that they would be singing formal songs even if the work were an ordinary drama. Thus I am driven to maintain the paradox that music is free precisely where the theorists of declamation call it formal, and that it is trammelled by what is commonly called free declamation. I have recently had a surprising experience of the practical facts of the case. I have written a voluminous opera to a text by an English poet who has unlimited command of metre. From the outset of my composition I was determined both to accept the strictest Wagnerian theories of declamation and at the same time to throw my whole invention into fastidiously musical designs. I found that the declamation could in no wise be attained through the designs, but that my best designs from a purely musical point of view could all be accurately attained through the declamation; and so I came to realize that, even in purely instrumental music, the composer should be primarily a rhetorician. This I ought to have known from the outset, but I could not have expected, what I have since found, that on the revision of the translation of the text into German the passages where the singers were bound to the clearest lyric forms were the easiest to translate. I expected that where I was merely declamatory the translation could easily afford to consider nothing but German sense and idiom, since I was alive and ready to make new musical declamation for it. I found, on the contrary, that these passages were extremely difficult. I was by no means in love with my most complex declamation and was often glad to find something simpler; but the freedom of alternatives was always greatest where the music was most straightforward. The problems of translating English into German are very different from those of translating German into English, for English is enormously more varied and flexible in its accentuation. If I had ever had a patronizing critical attitude towards Wagner I should have soon been cured of it, and my already great respect for Frederick Jameson's English translation of *The Ring* became a veneration second only to that which I have for Wagner himself.

Under the influence of the renascence of sixteenth-century music, current criticism is now happily outgrowing the crude dance-rhythm emphasis which, together with the hard accentual tendencies of the German language, made the official Wagnerian-Hugo Wolf theories of declamation so inferior to the practice of those composers. The latest phase of this crudity is also beginning to wane, as the modern composer comes to realize that his notation of ostensibly free and irregular rhythms is the bane of orchestral conductors and players, and that to write a bar of five quavers followed by a bar of six and a bar of three and another single quaver and the *Luftpause* is no better than the riding of a frightened boy tugging at the mouth of a race-horse in a chaos of London traffic. In a later edition of one of his earlier works Stravinsky has substituted ordinary equidistant bars of suitable average metre for his original convulsive notation. The difference this makes to the orchestra and conductor is that the work can be perfectly rehearsed in a quarter of the time; and the naïve listener will probably notice that the performance is better than it used to be. Conversely, classical music could easily become fantastically difficult for conductors and orchestras if the framework of its uniform bars were changed, as it were, from rectangular co-ordinates to some attempt to follow the shapes of its 'islands and capes' by Gaussian co-ordinates.

Our sense of musical rhetoric must not be interfered with by confusion between practical methods and aesthetic results. All art and all rhetoric allow their elements to exercise themselves in apparently free enjoyment of their capacities, each coming to its own climax at its own time, while the governing, creative power chooses its opportunity for bringing several or all the elements to a supreme climax at the one right moment. Thus, in the simplest melody we have the high note, the long note, the syncopated note, the sensitive harmony, and the muscular or jog-trot accent. Why should these always come together, and what merit is there in a theory which sets the jog-trot accent in authority over all the others? Certainly more merit than in the later theory that seeks for freedom in the irresponsible tyranny of jogs that are too irregular to trot.

The elements that I have so far described are those that are manifest in detail within the scope of melody. When we come to the elements of larger musical forms the power of musical rhetoric is increased far beyond what the word 'rhetoric' can be conveniently stretched to include. Demosthenes may be said to have magnified the details of rhetoric under a microscope when he defined its three elements as 'action, action, and action'. He thus gives us a good classical excuse for extending the scope of the word in the opposite way. Let us use a telescope and regard the qualities of drama and musical architecture as rhetoric on a large scale. We shall then not need the apparatus of Wagnerian drama to see in the exactness, the timing, and the freedom of a symphonic recapitulation the same enormous dramatic power that overwhelms us when Isolde's *Liebestod* reproduces a hundred bars of her love-duet with Tristan, or when in *Götterdämmerung* Siegfried's reminiscences of his adventures in the forest with Mime and the dragon, and of the message of the bird pass, hardly interrupted by the assassin's stroke, into the music of Brünnhilde's awakening as his full memory returns in death.

Whether a musical form is free or mechanical is not a matter to be measured by statistics or settled by historic precedent or habit. In the largest and most free compositions there may or may not be passages where the composer might as well entrust one or several pages to a copyist; but we must beware of all short cuts of criticism that refer these passages to convention or to the convenience of the composer. The trivial accident of genius outweighs all the historic causes and labour-saving origins that may help or hinder the production of works of art. The imaginative composer probably does not as a matter of practical necessity spend time in measuring the precise effect of a repetition or recapitulation; but his imagination is alert even where he is saving himself trouble. There is no essential difference between the freedom of musical cloudscapes like Palestrina's *Stabat Mater* and Bach's Chromatic Fantasia, where there are neither themes nor polyphony, and the freedom of the first movement of Beethoven's 'Eroica' Symphony, in which the portion faithfully recapitulated is in point of time almost exactly the length of Isolde's *Liebestod*. The composer cannot leave such sections to be filled in by the copyist, because when he comes to fill them in himself his very pulse proves sensitive to the need for expressing the minute differences between an experience first felt and the experience renewed in the conflicting lights of twilight memory and new daylight.

On this matter of recapitulation Philipp Emanuel Bach and Haydn have given us priceless illustrations of the difference between intelligent theory and the workings of a higher order of genius that gratefully accepts the theory but penetrates through it to the truth. I have often had occasion to point out that it is a mistake to regard Philipp Emanuel Bach as the connecting link between the styles of his father and those of Mozart and Haydn. Not even his own testimony, in a personal message that Haydn was the one younger composer who understood him, can alter the fact that the essence of the Haydn-Mozart styles is even more dramatic than the operatic reforms of Gluck—that, in fact, the dramatic power and concentration of purely instrumental music in the sonata style far transcends anything that even Wagner could put upon the stage. It was not Philipp Emanuel Bach who achieved any pioneer work in this direction, but the far milder and less distinguished Johann Christian Bach, who settled in London and who supplied the art of music, both in operas and in symphonies, with the actual histrionic gestures that Mozart and Haydn used, often conventionally enough, but always to dramatic purpose. Philipp Emanuel Bach's style was, indeed, rhetorical, but tended more and more towards sentimental lyricism, and the invention of his later years on which he most prided himself was that of the *Sonaten mit veränderten Reprisen*—that is to say, sonatas in which not merely the recapitulation but the actual repeats were written out in full in order that the ornamental details might be changed. The normal sonata form had, in fact, swelled itself out from the scheme of a melody that fell into two portions, each of which was repeated. The first portion had ended with a definite close and possibly a new theme in the dominant. Apart from the prescribed repetition of the portions, as indicated by a repeat mark, the second part ends with a recapitulation which reproduces the dominant material of the first part in the tonic. It would be impossible to devise anything more paralysing to a dramatic, as distinguished from a merely rhetorical, style than Philipp Emanuel's just mentioned great innovation; and, even in quick movements, he has often quite miscalculated the effect of wading through the second part in both its not very plain penny version and its tuppence-coloured version. The sonatas with varied repeats are always charming and distinguished; but in the long run we cease to be able to tell one theme from another. Haydn imitated this form in several of his most characteristic slow movements, the most beautiful of which exists in two versions in one of his last symphonies, and, without repeat, in a trio in F sharp minor. In the symphony the repeat is written out in full to vary, not the orchestration, but the ornamentation. In no case does Haydn repeat the second part at all. He makes his recapitulation a compromise between the two versions; nor does Haydn ever apply the device to anything but an essentially lyric slow movement. I only wish that I were able to quote such examples in full, but that is always the standing obstacle to illustrating anything really important about larger musical forms in a lecture. I should want at least a quarter of an hour to display the suicidal elegance of Philipp Emanuel Bach's thought, and another six minutes to show Haydn's advance upon it; and then you would, if I played at all decently, enjoy your Philipp Emanuel Bach in spite of all I could say against it, and your musical palate would be in no condition to appreciate the subtle difference between it and the Haydn.

MUSICAL SHAPES

BOTH in the composition and the criticism of music, recent tendencies have shown a decided reluctance to face the fact that the art of music gained enormously in scope and in dramatic intensity when the focus of attention was withdrawn from the texture of the music and directed to the external shape. The immediate effect of this change of view was to make music pass through a trivial phase. Bach would sometimes propose as a kind of holiday jaunt an excursion to Dresden to listen to the *divertissements* which Hasse was producing there: music of which the texture was cheap, though the melodies were elegant enough and the sound anything but nasty. Philipp Emanuel Bach after his father's death agreed with Burney in professing a definite revolt against elaborate polyphony, and remarked that composers like Hasse were able to produce more euphony out of the simplest homophonic orchestral harmony than older composers could produce with the most imposing multiplicity of parts. As I showed at the end of my last lecture, Philipp Emanuel was so completely unconscious of any more radical revolution in music that of all his achievements he was most proud of his invention of the sonata with varied repeats: a device that concentrated attention on the superficial details of ornament which had become subject to the extempore impulses of singers and players, and which he proposed henceforth to prescribe accurately as essential parts of the composer's inspiration. I have shown how Haydn appreciated not only the merits but the limitations of this line of progress, and imitated Philipp Emanuel Bach only in the first halves of lyrical slow movements. Philipp Emanuel's comment on the euphony of the simple orchestration of Hasse and other contemporaries becomes more instructive than he realized when we see it in the light of two contemporary facts. First, there is the fact that he deplores the decay of the art of continuo-playing—the art of supplying on the harpsichord, or preferably the pianoforte, a completely unobtrusive background to the written harmony of the orchestral instruments: secondly, in his own symphonies, though he supplies a figured bass to the continuo-player, he directs that fully half the symphony should be played *tasto solo*—that is to say, that the continuo-player should play nothing but the bass notes. Actually, he is himself a pioneer in the style in which the orchestra does its own domestic service and makes the continuo-player obsolete. A far more illuminating expression of the change that had already come over music is Gluck's remark, in his famous preface to *Alceste*, that the instruments should be employed in proportion to the dramatic passions of the situation. What Gluck is taking for granted is that hitherto all groups of orchestral instruments were used in a pattern. If Sebastian Bach accompanies an aria by strings and an oboe, the strings will have throughout the aria some valuable design supporting a flowing melody for the oboe; but the *locus classicus* for Gluck's use of strings and oboe is the passage where Agamemnon, protesting against the Gods' command that he should sacrifice his daughter, declaims 'J'entends retentir dans mon âme le cri plaintif de la Nature', while the strings accompany with the merest palpitation and the oboe contributes *le cri plaintif* very simply stylized, and punctuated by something like sobbing in pizzicato bass notes. The effect of the texture is as dramatic and thrilling as anything in Wagner; but the textures need not have any such value as long as they change. Music can henceforth get the highest artistic values from textures which would be intrinsically worthless but for the fact that the art is at liberty to change them.

In the latter half of the nineteenth century two circumstances helped to produce what has now developed into a grotesque revolt of precious criticism against the working hypotheses of the art which culminated in Beethoven. It was quite obvious that immensely powerful works, such as Bach's Toccata in F, produce much of their cumulative effect by their refusal to change their texture. In fact, Beethoven cannot and will not, even in the Ninth Symphony, maintain any musical texture uninterrupted for a quarter of the length of the F major Toccata. At the other extreme of dramatic music Wagner has taught us to appreciate the piling up of musical reiterations to an extent that transcends not only Beethoven but the severest cumulative schemes of Bach. To his contemporaries Wagner seemed empty in comparison with Beethoven. To Beethoven's contemporaries passages like the dozen bars of contrary-motion thirds in the andante of the C minor Symphony sounded as they would sound to you and me if we did not recognize them apart from their context and were told to refer them to the style of Mozart.

Having thus arrived at the style of Mozart, let us

now accept the F major Toccata of Bach, and let us associate Mozart with the opening of one of his most cheerful finales. In these circumstances perhaps you may choose to take up the position of the superior person who nowadays makes it a point of conscience and of fashion to regard Mozart, Haydn, and Beethoven as representing a deplorable intrusion of the trivialities of jazz into what ought to have remained the inviolable sanctuary of serious art. I venture to believe that I have described this attitude quite as fairly as its own representatives. I call it silly.

The fundamental fact that we must now bear in mind is that music after the time of Bach became inveterately dramatic; that in so doing it for some time and for some aspects appeared to lose much of its architectural power; that it soon gained, even in architectural power, immeasurably more than it lost; and that it ceased to depend upon extensive material for its texture.

The musical experiences which I have tried to summarize in my first two lectures will have prepared you to realize that the external shapes of music ought not to be conceived as pre-existing moulds into which the composer has to pack his materials. Life is too short and art too long for us to refuse the help of generalizations. But we must generalize from a detailed experience of the behaviour of individual works, and must not try to explain that behaviour by the generalization. As I pointed out in my second lecture, the anomaly in the fourth entry of Bach's C sharp minor Fugue might very well be supposed to illustrate a law if that fugue were the only one that we knew. Beethoven's Sonata in B flat, op. 22, is the most normal of all his works in the sense that it is his nearest approximation to the average procedures of sonata form. His C sharp minor Quartet is so unique in all points that it is popularly supposed to be quite improvisatorial. I once devoted a long article in *Music and Letters* to the demonstration that the Sonata, op. 22, was free in the sense that it proved itself perfectly justified in conforming to average procedures, and that the C sharp minor Quartet was the strictest of all Beethoven's works, if by strictness we mean the necessity of the material to be shaped as it is.

We can actually find an art-form of which even the external hypothesis identifies the form with the matter. Such a form is that of the figured chorale for a definite number of parts each of which makes fugue-texture of the successive clauses of the chorale-tune, with or without a leading part which delivers the whole tune slowly, phrase by phrase. There is nothing to prevent a capable contrapuntist from grinding out such compositions by the same sort of machinery as that which produces commercial correspondence, and I confess that the complete works of Praetorius, some forty-odd volumes of which are occupied mainly with exercises in this form, have so far failed to engage my attention as perhaps they might have done when I was younger and more patient. Certainly a note-for-note correspondence between matter and form can be achieved in figured chorales without the inspiration of genius; but Sweelinck and Bach achieved it in terms of the highest genius, and in such cases it is not uninteresting to speculate whether the rhetoric might not have created the crystalline mechanism of the form instead of the mechanism admitting the rhetoric. As a practical matter the question is absurd. The composer knew his chorale tune before he crystallized it, and in most cases the tune is not his own composition. My leading cases, which I have cited in other lectures than the present course, are a Psalm by Sweelinck on the tune which we now know as the Old Hundredth and Bach's four-part setting of *Aus tiefer Noth* for organ.

I cannot quote the Bach example here, but the statistical facts of it are that the majority of its actual notes are accounted for by its form, and that the rest are grammatically necessary to the harmonic sense. The interesting aesthetic question is: what is the difference between this composition and a mere academic exercise, such as might reasonably be prescribed to a candidate for a musical degree? The obvious answer is the correct pious opinion that the examiners for the musical degree ought to be satisfied by smoothness and correctness, whereas Bach's composition is a masterpiece of pathetic rhetoric. Thence arises the deeper but quite unpractical question whether the rhetoric might not itself have existed first and sufficed to produce the accurate crystalline form. This question is not so nonsensical as it might seem; for, as a matter of fact, Martin Luther's tune was inspired by the metrical *De Profundis* to which he composed it, and his choice of the Phrygian mode is the deliberate choice of a very definite and emotional harmonic system. It is not a very long step from such a system to a polyphony based on the notes of the melody, and if the melody had been Bach's own there might already have been some conscious preference for turns of phrase that would be easy to handle in

47

fugue-texture. And so we have already reached the point at which a quite elaborate and apparently rigid art-form might be practically forced upon a composer by rhetorical necessity instead of being a pre-existing mould to which he must adapt his thoughts.

The Sweelinck Psalm, *Or sus, serviteurs du Seigneur* (a specially inspired item in four volumes of a more than complete polyphonic metrical Psalter), is important to my present argument for a different reason. Of all the pastimes of musical analysis, the easiest is the identifying of melodic figures. An uncontrolled imagination—that is to say, an unimaginative mind—can pursue this to results as fantastic as any Baconian cipher, and composers themselves may be misled by it. My own firm belief, which I take liberty to impart to my students as a pile-driven orthodoxy, is that no sane composer makes his compositions depend for any aesthetic value upon remote melodic derivations, or upon anything in the music which needs to be seen by the eye as well as heard by the ear. There is no harm in merely cryptographic external devices. We have already seen that, especially in primitive forms of art, many quite external and sometimes abstruse mechanical devices may precipitate the highest art, as a cat's-cradle of thread or wire shape may gather crystals round it, or a particle of grit may stimulate the oyster to build a pearl. The composer is inevitably more conscious of the irritating or precipitating impulse of his work than the oyster; and in advanced forms of art it is possible for a great master of form and counterpoint to use quite elaborate external cryptographic and mechanical devices without feeling any hindrance to the natural flow of his real

48

thoughts. Nevertheless, it is important that neither critics nor composers should be misled by false doctrines as to the nature and purpose of their technique; and few among false musical doctrines are more dangerous than the theory that music is built up from figures. The teaching of composition and the understanding of music would be greatly advanced if a law were made forbidding the assertion that Beethoven's C minor Symphony is founded upon a figure of four notes. Melodies are not built up out of figures. They are large musical objects which are divisible into figures. The initial idea of Beethoven's C minor Symphony is not its first four notes. What sounds like half the opening statement is not really so: the second half leads continuously into wider issues.

The figure may stand for an idea to much the same extent as a single word; and figures may develop from one idea to another, not by mechanism, but by associations and contexts which explain themselves with a cogency quite unattainable by arbitrary mechanisms. We must not be misled by appearances. Many melodies will invert into equally beautiful and natural melodies; and the character of the inversion may be novel to the ear when the appearance of the written notes may be a mere mirror-effect to the eye. If a composer has devoted much time to the polyphonic art-forms he may have a tendency to invent melodies that will invert well. Purcell, Bach, Mozart, and Brahms are composers with whom inverted themes constantly pass for natural ones. Beethoven's for the most part would not; and so he seldom troubles to use the device.

49

Obviously there is no reason to invert a theme that would become ugly by the process, and there is no fallacy of criticism more childish than that which imputes ingenuity to the device, even by way of admiration for beautiful examples or by way of excuse for bad ones. Inversion, like most of the devices used in fugues, happens to be a mechanical way of treating a melody. The breaking up of a melody into smaller figures, the alteration of these figures, and the re-distribution of them into new melodies are not rigid devices; but, like inversion, they may be good or bad. Nothing is easier than to derive any musical idea whatever from any other musical idea; and a long chain of such derivations is often supposed to em-body the logic of music. In itself it can give us no security that it is more logical than a series of puns. Our researches for the logic of music must be deeper and wider.

To illustrate some true musical logic, let me return to Sweelinck's setting of the tune known as the Old Hundredth. The very great musician who introduced me to this masterpiece was quite surprised when I discovered that the tune was the Old Hundredth. The fact added something not wholly negligible to our enjoyment of the music; and the musical perfection would be definitely impaired if we sang the work to a translation which failed to solve the difficult problem produced by the elisions of French prosody. According-ing to the unsound doctrine which I would like to forbid, Sweelinck's music is built up of various figures. The truth, on the contrary, is that the words spontaneously break up the Old Hundredth into figures corresponding respectively with:

Or sus
Serviteurs du Seigneur
Qui nuict et jour
En son honneur
Dedans sa maison le servez
Louez-l(e)
Et son nom
Eslevez.

For the translator the last line presents a difficulty, because *louez-le* becomes a complete figure with a full-sized note for the final syllable *le*, whereas in the verse that syllable is elided into *et son nom*. You see, however, that all this exquisite figure-work comes of the merest common-sense treatment of the words. The music will not disappear if sung to a bad translation. But I very much doubt whether it could have been produced by the author of a treatise on organ-playing which some forty years ago caused unholy hilarity among reviewers, especially because of its naïve illustration of how, say, twelve notes could be developed in twenty-two versions by docking it note by note one way until only the first note was left and the other way until only the last note was left, on which the obvious comment was that the author had omitted the two most desirable transformations of all: namely, the results of docking it of all twelve notes.

The understanding of Wagner has on the whole been hindered more than it has been helped by the ease with which his enormous structures can be analysed into small figures naturally inseparable from the dramatic occasions in which they originated. Wagner himself did not build up from fragments

He thought in musical ideas as enormous as the processes of his drama. A leitmotive may be identified by two notes. You can trace the whimpering of Mime in Alberich's aspirations to world-power; only you had better not believe this unless Wagner has led you continuously from one idea to the other. He can lead you more directly to Alberich's designs from the innocent babbling of the Rhine-maidens; and his darkest dreams will transform themselves just as easily into the sumptuous glory of Valhalla.

In all these transformations Wagner is at the top of his form. In so huge a work as *The Ring* we need not be surprised that the inspiration which produces this natural system of leitmotive should now and then fail, and be replaced by an inferior kind of artificial derivation on the mental plane of those who believe that Wagnerian music-drama can be built up from scraps of leitmotive. I can, however, recall only one instance of such a failure, and that is the attempt to turn the young Siegfried's horn-theme into an expression of grown-up manhood. You have only to compare this with such genuine transformations as pervade the works of Brahms and are far too natural there to attract the notice of commentators, and you will at once see the difference between genius at its most *genial* and genius reduced by fatigue to dullness and artificiality.

I must now change the subject and deal with the broad distinction between music that attracts attention chiefly to its texture and music that expresses itself mainly by its shape. Both listeners and composers are well advised to attend chiefly to the texture of music; for in works that move in time some of the worst hindrances to enjoyment and understanding arise from false ideas of the powers and conditions of memory. The one safe way of listening to music, or to anything that moves in time, is to give your attention to what is going on all the time. Your memory and hence your capacity for expectation and surprise will be at their best when left alone. You will then listen to Palestrina without expecting impossibilities; and the solid realities of his music will then surprise you like the discovery that a mystic philosophy can be a practical guide to life.

With works that depend more concretely on your powers of memory much will escape you at a first hearing; but if you simply enjoy the texture the whole will not have escaped you, as it certainly would if you had attempted to grasp it. It is the whole that will vibrate in your memory. (Why, oh why, do our poets speak only of the music of *soft* voices, with an occasional diversion to the trumpet's loud clangour?) But the larger shapes of music are easy to describe, and the description produces in us the notion that these shapes exist like maps, and can be so apprehended in the musical consciousness. This has become a doctrine to which weighty support has been given by a letter ascribed to Mozart, in which he says that he imagines his compositions existing timelessly in that way; so that his mind takes them in as the eye appreciates a design in a single *coup d'œil*. I believe that that letter has been proved to be a fantasia by Rochlitz. In any case, we are all apt to imagine well-sounding things of that sort. As a child I was firmly under the belief that I visualized the scores of everything I heard; until a few searching questions from Joachim convinced me, not only that I did not, but that my powers of visualizing are very poor, and that all that happened when I listened to a score was that I had a general visual impression of printed music, which satisfied me perfectly as long as I didn't trouble to read it. But there is a certain analogy between our power of seeing a shape in space and our apprehension of musical shapes. If I am not mistaken, the metaphysical notion that is relevant to this power is the 'specious present'. This I will not attempt to define technically, but I take it to mean any portion of time which, for one reason or another, we cannot conveniently separate into past, present, and future. You cannot articulate a syllable in less than a tenth of a second, though it is easy enough to play runs and arpeggios the individual complete notes of which are shorter than the vibrations of the lowest musical sounds. But, though prosody is highly sensitive to the varying lengths of single syllables, and though a heavy single syllable such as 'strength' may take as long to pronounce as three light syllables, we naturally think of it as instantaneous rather than as having a beginning, a middle, and an end.

Now with music this kind of specious present is very extensive. For the average naïve modern listener it includes as much time as is needed for the impression that a phrase is tuneful. While a tune is completing its symmetry the mind follows it expectantly from point to point, comparing the past with the present and anticipating the future, but if the phrase is memorable to a normal musical mind it thereafter vibrates in the memory as a unit. Such an example is far larger than anything that Palestrina would so apprehend. His specious present is very much larger than that of spoken language, but not of a totally different order. Beethoven's tune is shorter than the melody of a Gregorian hymn, but its obvious symmetry would offend Palestrina as trivial, not because Palestrina has anything in common with the superior persons who think so to-day, but because Palestrina's way of treating such a melody would be to develop its individual figures one by one in fugue, and to represent the continuous melody, if at all, in notes of enormous length.

With Palestrina the specious present, if that is the correct term, usually lasts from one musical accent to the next, and is thus only as much longer than that of words as the music is slower than the rate of speech. Music must, in fact, pass through humbler and more trivial phases while it learns to build larger forms and to train the mind to grasp them. Even in the art of Bach the forms that are defined by shape are lighter than those which depend on texture. They are typified by the dance-forms of his suites; and they are not greatly expanded from the dimensions of a single melody.

At this point it becomes convenient to use the word 'form' in generalized contrast with the word 'texture'. In this sense the texture of music is the art which arises from the character of voices and instruments, and which ranges from the highest kinds of counterpoint downwards to the simplest formulas of accompaniment. Form, on the other hand, is in the first instance melody writ large; and it ranges from the shape of a single complete tune at least as far as designs like the first movement of Beethoven's Fifth

Pianoforte Concerto and of his 'Eroica' Symphony and Ninth Symphony. My own belief is that this notion of form is ultimately applicable to the whole of Wagner's *Ring*. And I am seriously inclined to attempt to give an account of that tetralogy as a musical composition. For it seems to me that the most neglected aspect of Wagner's art is that which views it as the work of a musical composer.

If form is melody writ large, the most crucial point is that at which the music passes beyond the dimensions of a single melody. For Bach, the principal ways in which melodic form expands are: first, the spacing out of a figured chorale; and second, the ritornello of an aria or concerto. The figured chorale is obviously a texture form. In the first chorus of the *Matthew Passion* the orchestra propounds a concerto-ritornello in double fugue, which is developed by an antiphonal double choir and surmounted by a slow chorale sung by a third choir and poised above the whole in a foreign key, like a cathedral dome seen at an unexpected angle.

We need not have been brought up since infancy like Bach's listeners to recognize the chorale tune. By the time we know the chorus fairly well the music will have convinced us that its length and proportions are determined precisely by that tune set in the framework of the ritornello. The principle of the ritornello, which governs all arias and concertos, is that the orchestra begins with a complete musical paragraph, and that the one or more solo instruments or voices discuss the materials of this paragraph, together with more or less new material, expanding freely until capped at climaxes in one key and another by the re-entry of the orchestra with the ritornello; until a circle of related keys has been covered and the time has come for final emphasis in the home tonic, upon which the original ritornello finishes the design.

This type of form thus covers its ground like the ox-hide which the founders of Carthage cut into so many strips that it sufficed to define the limits of their city. There are other ways in which melodic forms can expand, but these other ways lead beyond the conception of a single melody. The criterion I wish to make clear is one that I have not yet seen properly emphasized. In most of the orthodox statements about form it is hopelessly obscured by obvious external appearances. In English terminology the ambiguous word 'subject' has created disastrous misunderstandings in every musical form. We are now concerned with the radical difference between a suite movement of Bach, which I would prefer to describe as essentially decorative, lyric, or, if you like, purely melodic, and a sonata movement by Haydn, of which the tendency is, even in early examples, inveterately dramatic. My criterion has only an accidental connexion with the number of different themes or subjects present in a composition, though I cannot deny that a lyric, or decorative, work is likely to be quite happy with only one theme, and that a dramatic work will probably need at least two. But for this very reason the difference between a decorative and a dramatic work could best be illustrated by an example in which Bach is unable to be polyphonic and is using two clearly contrasted themes, and an example from Haydn which is polyphonic from beginning to end and concentrated entirely on a single theme. The essential difference between these two kinds of music lies, not in where new themes begin, but in whether the music moves so far that its starting-point disappears below the horizon. Even with Bach's greatest designs the key of the opening —or, as I find it convenient to call it, the home tonic —is in relation to the other keys as the horses in the days of chivalry are to knights in armour. As Alice remarked when the Red Knight and the White Knight were fighting, their horses let them get on and off as if they were tables. The changes of key in such a mighty design as the first chorus of the *Matthew Passion* are determined first by the bounds of the opening ritornello, which, though fugal in texture, is a single paragraph of melody; and when the chorale tune supervenes, it slightly enlarges the harmonic range by being itself pitched in another key. This produces a wider swing of the harmonic pendulum; but it produces neither means nor necessity for emphasis on returns to the home tonic. Such emphasis is needed only to round off the whole design. And this is achieved by making the double chorus sing the opening ritornello after the end of the chorale has been cunningly harmonized so as to close in the home tonic.

Not such are the modulations of music on the dramatic basis established by Haydn and Mozart. The importance of a change of key depends, not on its remoteness, but on whether it is a colour-effect in the course of a melody or a dramatic action which has caused the home tonic to disappear below the horizon. Composers long before Beethoven were often fond of experimenting with brilliant changes of key. Such experiments may almost be reckoned among the means by which the founders of classical tonality established the normal solidity of their harmony; but between such colour-effects and the most ordinary sonata-like establishment of the orthodox dominant, or the relative major, there is as much difference as there is between looking at pictures of foreign places in an album and travelling, bag and baggage, to spend the night in another house. Similarly, the return to the home tonic becomes a matter of dramatic importance. As I have often had reason to point out in other connexions, it normally means a return to things which we have learnt to associate with the home tonic. Composers with a grasp of musical psychology do not expect us to recognize the home tonic as a mere matter of absolute pitch. And it may even be doubtful whether after a wide range of modulations the absolute pitch of the tonic would remain constant if the intonation were mathematically perfect instead of being tempered to the notes of instruments with a finite number of notes.

The architectural symmetries into which music naturally grows have produced two main types of large musical shape. These originate in two types of melody which have received the unfortunate and superficial names of 'binary' and 'ternary'. In the binary form the first part ends elsewhere than on the tonic and the second part ends on the tonic with more or less effect of symmetrical balance with the end of the first part. In the ternary form the first part ends in the tonic; and, as the second part necessarily ends likewise, it often recapitulates the whole of the first part after having begun with something different.

Thus, the ternary form becomes typified with a scheme which may be symbolized as A B A, whereas the binary form is not so amenable to such a division unless the element of recapitulation is very strong. Hence, many theorists have been tempted to argue that, as Sir Henry Hadow has put it in his primer on sonata form, 'we have here a serious case of cross-classification', and that the sonata-scheme of exposition, development, and recapitulation is itself ternary. The fact is that we have here, not a serious case of cross-classification at all, but a much more serious confusion between time and space.

All essentially maplike terms of musical form are *a priori* nonsensical. The power of prophecy in the normal musical listener is not negligible; but it ought to rest on what the music tells him from point to point in the individual work, and not upon statistical information compiled from other works. When you have heard the first half of a binary composition you have no legitimate means of guessing that the rest will consist merely of a second half, or of a second and third. Nor have you any means of knowing from the first half of a so-called ternary form that the rest is going to consist of two other portions; and, as a matter of fact, the ternary forms are quite apt to produce five or six other portions. I have never known, and never shall know, enough Greek to devise proper terms for the two main types of musical form. The terms must be such as will describe what we can know at the decisive moment when the music shows its type. This decisive moment is recognizable at the end of the first section. That section is evidently either complete or incomplete. If it has ended elsewhere than on or in the tonic, it is incomplete and the organization is what is commonly called binary. If it is complete, then it is self-evidently part of a scheme the tendency of which is rather to alternate comparatively complete objects than to devote itself wholly to highly organized developments. The simplest case of such an alternation may be represented by the formula A B A; and the natural way to expand this is to make a rondo with a theme A alternating with episodes, as A B, A C, &c.

On a small scale both the binary and the ternary schemes may be emphasized by repeating their parts; but simple experience shows that for the purposes of repetition both of them fall into two parts, and that nothing can be more inept than to treat the portions of a so-called ternary melody otherwise than as A B A. This is self-evident where we have a true single ternary melody in which, though A is complete, B is a digression the function of which is to move away from A in order to return to it. If B has its own completeness, then we are no longer sure that we are dealing with a single melody; and we may as well draw some distinction between the genuine A B A form of a single melody and the juxtaposition of such complete things as a minuet and trio each with its own form, binary or ternary, and with the minuet repeated after the trio. Long before these forms have expanded either in length or dramatic concentration to the tremendous issues of sonatas and symphonies, I have lost interest in their terminology. All that concerns me is that, when the first section of a work has defined itself decisively as incomplete, I expect a more continuous and higher type of organization than when it has defined itself as complete. Hence, if Beethoven begins with a broad melody, I naturally enjoy the naïve listener's pleasure in it without worrying whether it is going to be a rondo or an effort in serious sonata form. My conviction that it is dealing with weightier issues will grow as the theme grows beyond the squareness of a rondo tune.

But I shall not worry about the classification of border-line cases. If a rondo has a rather businesslike theme, which has a shortened return after its first episode and passes into a serious development instead of into a duller formal episode, I shall not consider myself involved in a serious case of cross-classification, but shall take the music as I find it. All the great composers learnt from their predecessors and contemporaries, but all of them have had their own habits. Haydn and Mozart remained radically different, even where they learnt most from each other, and much of the enormous increase of Beethoven's range of form might be defined as the result of an integration of Mozart's forms with Haydn's. We may accuse Beethoven of imitating Mozart in his Septet and in his Quintet for pianoforte and wind instruments, but Mozart's powers of form reappear in their true Olympian majesty in Beethoven's middle and later works, which no one has ever dreamt of calling Mozartian.

It is neither an unmixed blessing nor a disaster that we can trace a clear line of historic development in the expansion of two types of single melody into the powerful dramatic forms of the sonata style, by internal expansion of the whole binary melody into the serious sonata form, by multiplication of the ternary melody into the rondo with several episodes, and by the merging of the one type into the other. Obviously the progress of these developments implies the obsolescence of what the naïve listener recognizes as tunefulness, yet academicism descends to its lowest vulgarity when it encourages the notion that melody is an aspect of music which in these days of travel by rail and aircraft is as obsolete as horse traffic. I will not give the name of a recent famous composer who defended his conscientious avoidance of tunefulness by this illustration.

The fallacy is the same as that which believes that Wagnerian opera can be built up from its leitmotives. Tunefulness is a quality which depends mainly upon the experience of the listener. If his experience is so small as to be disturbed by any breach of eight-bar symmetry, Palestrina's melodic range will be too short for him, though, on the other hand, the somnolent eight-bar symmetries of jazz may leave him satisfied with the tunefulness of instruments of mere percussion. A highly trained musician will at once recognize tunefulness in such an irregular melody as that of the slow movement of Brahms's Second Symphony, but will not expect to know all about it until the whole movement is finished. A less experienced musician may be misled by the more familiar idioms of Mozart to think that he has something less abstruse in the slow movement of Mozart's G minor Quintet. In the last resort the coherence of a composition as large as Wagner's *Ring* is essentially the coherence, not of melody in general, but of *a* melody. With the pioneer work of great interpreters such as Joachim and Casals, followed up by the courageous enterprise on a vast scale of the leaders of musical broadcasting, Bach has become a genuinely popular composer. One of his qualities that strikes the naïve listener and has earned the approval of persons over-ready in forming aesthetic theories on the first music they happen to understand is that most of Bach's works seem to end within their own length. With very rare exceptions, it is practically impossible for Bach to end a composition otherwise than with the end of a theme. You cannot conceive that any movement of the B minor Mass should need some merely architectural chords to complete it; but, when musicians regard the last forty-odd bars of Beethoven's C minor Symphony as a meaningless noise they are as far from the truth as the most naïve listener to whom a fugue is a tuneless chaos. These forty bars are meaningless without the rest of the symphony, but the symphony ends as truly within its own length as the 'Et in terra pax' of the B minor Mass.

By this time you will be ready to pardon me for leaving this statement as a dogmatic assertion. There are practical limits to the choice of things that a lecturer can prove. Finality in a classical symphony is attained by quite different means from those which will achieve finality in a Bach chorus. I must suppose that you are ready to believe that, if form be melody writ large, a master like Beethoven is justified in measuring the length of these forty-odd bars in proportion to the whole symphony, as he would measure a pause on the sustained last note of a single tune. Far be it from me to impose Beethoven's authority, still less my authority, upon your musical experience. But it saves time to take for granted the correctness of

Beethoven's judgement in one of his most famous works. In a viva voce examination in English literature a candidate once defined Butler's *Analogy* as 'a sermon designed to prove the existence of the Creator'. Whereupon the examiner pointed out that, broad as the preacher's views might doubtless be, in a sermon the existence of the Creator was usually taken for granted.

ABSOLUTE MUSIC

ABSOLUTE music is a result which neither composers nor critics can understand until they have cleared their minds of all confusion with the processes that lead to it. I am by upbringing and inclination the most absolute of musicians, with a violent prejudice against all attempts to substitute verbal for musical ideas in the interpretation of music. Even the best-authenticated programme of a piece of confessedly descriptive instrumental music rouses in me a mood of bristling inattention, which I can often justify by evidences that it has roused a similar mood in the composer himself. In music, as in other arts, the conditions are rare in which external ideas can intrude without harm. The most favourable conditions are, as we have seen, those of primitive art, which I have illustrated by the type of crystallization precipitated upon a foreign body in a saturated solution. Troubles begin when artists become self-conscious and ready, like the centipede, to consider the snail's question of which foot should take the first step.

Absolute music must have been produced somehow. And it is highly improbable that its creators have abandoned the experience and emotions of human beings, before, during, and after the process of creation. What is absolute music when it has been achieved? The question, thus qualified, may profitably be answered with complete disregard of how the music has been achieved. There is no reason against calling Beethoven's 'Pastoral' Symphony absolute music, unless we can show that its thunderstorm and cuckoo and nightingale and other items of its programme are intrusive and destructive of its musical design; and this has never been shown by anybody who did not display extensive ignorance of the real principles of musical form, besides exactly the childish prejudices which he imputes to the mythical popular listener who is supposed to be attracted to the symphony by its programme. These childish prejudices prevented all sorts and conditions of 'listeners' from hearing the music of Beethoven's 'Pastoral' Symphony at its very first performance and ever since. They have no philosophical basis beyond the *a priori* notion that every idea expressible in words must be intrusive if it can be recognized in instrumental music. According to Beethoven, the 'Pastoral' Symphony is intended rather to express feelings than to paint pictures in sound. It does commit a certain amount of sound-painting, and does effectively remind the listener of the things that Beethoven mentions by title, and if we are to be annoyed by this we ought to be infuriated by the converse process. The pleasures of the country, if we have ever been capable of enjoying them, ought to be ruined for all conscientious absolute musicians because of the resemblances between bird-songs, thunderstorms, brooks, fine weather, &c., in this degradation of Beethoven's art. Evidently some people are so constructed, and they seem proud of it. The real question is whether, as absolute musicians, we are bound by our absolutism to regard Beethoven's simple rural pleasures as incompatible with pure music.

What things are incompatible with pure music?

This is as dangerous as most *a priori* questions, and it is inconveniently complicated by the human foolishness of *a priori* thinkers. The experience of Beethoven's 'Pastoral' Symphony shows that that foolishness is most stimulated by the imitating of sounds. Beethoven's thunder rouses more righteous indignation than his rainbow; and the indignation descends to the childishness which it would rebuke when it points out that Beethoven makes the lightning follow the thunderclaps. One must be experienced in thunderstorms, natural or musical, and in a very un-impressionable and statistical state of mind, if one can be positive as to which thunderclap belongs to which flash.

On the same level of infuriated *naïveté* is the historical research that discovers that Beethoven has plagiarized his programme from a 'pastoral' symphony by some other person. It is possible that both com-posers plagiarized the experience independently from natural sources. In any case, the earlier composer deserves credit for not having fallen into the invari-able booby-trap of second-rate artists : that of avoid-ance of the obvious. 'Oh, the little more, and how much it is! The little less, and what worlds away!' The exactly right seems obvious. The difference between it and the things which are worlds away may also seem obvious when the examples are there for com-parison; but even then it may be exceedingly difficult to define. If I am to risk an *a priori* statement as to what is most dangerously intrusive upon the absoluteness of music, I will boldly specify the pre-conceived absolute musical form. Let us never forget that we are concerned here with results and not with processes. Even for so manifest an innovator as Beethoven himself, it is practically convenient to have a generalized notion of sonata form. Examples of such form arise in every case from what the nature of their materials has in common; and the force of habit saves the composer an immense amount of labour. He has every reason for allowing that force free play, and, indeed, for regarding it as a function of the force of imagination that controls it, and that overrides all precedent as the nature of the material requires. In the 'Pastoral' Symphony Beethoven is making precisely the same use of his habitual enjoyment of the resources of musical forms as he is making of his enjoyment of life in the country. He enjoyed exactly the same freedom of mind when his idealization of Napoleon coincided with the composition of his 'Eroica' Symphony. Heroes and hero-worshippers must face death and mourning. In a symphony expressing heroic ideas in classical music the emotions associated with death and mourning will find their natural position in the slow movement. The question which thunderclap belongs to which flash of lightning is not nearly as silly as the notion that the 'Eroica' Symphony should be a chronological biography of a hero and should therefore put the funeral march at the end. In accordance with this notion the scherzo, of course, becomes an irrelevant intrusion forced upon Beethoven by the pedantries of absolute music, and the finale, which happens to be unique in its musical form, is inexplicable on any theory, either of programme-music or of *a priori* structure. In the last resort, there is very little to choose between the silliness of trying to explain the

'Eroica' Symphony either as illustrating the life of Napoleon or as illustrating conformity to an *a priori* sonata form. On the whole the *a priori* sonata view leads to the fewest blunders and is not as manifestly illiterate as the biographical view. The only sane view is that which treats the 'Eroica' Symphony as an individual work of art and accepts all deviations from precedent as things existing in their own musical rights.

Of late years both critics and composers have become increasingly conscious of external influences on music. I decline to speak respectfully of recent attempts to find programmes for everything Beethoven ever wrote. Most people are agreed in hoping that the climax of silliness has been reached in a recent attempt to identify Beethoven's Sonata, op. 106, with the story of Joan of Arc: whether historical or as seen through the eyes of Schiller, Mark Twain, Shaw, or the author of the theory I neither know nor care. Beethoven gave a kind of sanction to all manner of speculations by saying that he always had a *Bild* in his mind when he composed. Fortunately for him, and unfortunately for those whose mother tongue is not German, the word *Bild* is of untranslatable generality and particularity. It is difficult to allow it to mean less than 'idea', and it certainly need not mean anything more precise than 'image'. But Beethoven had the sense to leave our enjoyment of his music untrammelled by words; and, in fact, it was his own imagination that he also left untrammelled when he refrained from putting into words the *Bild* which inspired him. Certainly, in the cases where he has committed himself, his indiscretion has obstructed the musical view even more effectively than recent purveyors of programmes can do by interposing Joan of Arc between us and the Sonata, op. 106. He and we have suffered a certain amount from his poor, much abused friend Schindler, who devoted himself to Beethoven with a dog-like fidelity, but who had not the genius of Boswell, and whose faithful services sometimes provoked Beethoven to a different kind of canine reaction. When Schindler questioned Beethoven about the meaning of his music, Beethoven's answers usually resembled those of a dog to the clatter of a tin pan tied to his tail. As to the meaning of his D minor Sonata, he advised Schindler to read Shakespeare's *Tempest*. The advice was perhaps not one of Beethoven's practical jokes: though I myself find both *The Tempest* and the D minor Sonata very much clearer when I do not compare them. But when Schindler asked Beethoven why he did not complete the Sonata, op. 111 with a triumphant finale, Beethoven said gruffly: 'There wasn't time'. Certainly there is no time to answer such questions. Why did Dante not complete the *Divine Comedy* with a triumphal fourth part after the *Paradiso*?

The real absoluteness of music lies simply in its untranslatability. I could have saved myself and you a great deal of trouble by substituting for my present lecture the reading of Andrew Bradley's inaugural lecture as Professor of Poetry at Oxford: a lecture, *Poetry for Poetry's Sake*, which I heard him deliver some forty years ago, and which without a single reference to music expressed and helped to formulate exactly my ideas on the absoluteness of music.

The general outcome of Bradley's doctrine is that

works of art digest their materials, and that the material before it is digested is not the same as it becomes when it is part of the work of art. I would venture to go so far as to say that few things are more indigestible by a work of art than a correct theory of art. The classical poet will describe sculpture as producing the illusion of life. It is poetical to say that the marble breathes; and it is highly unpoetical to explain that the sculptor is achieving something higher than the realistic illusion of a waxwork. The instinct for absolute purity in art is far too strong to be destroyed by the fact that normal occasions cause the art to derive its material from pre-existing externals; but we artists are gullible folk, and our strongest instincts are cruelly at the mercy of theorists who would cut off from us the normal occasions for the practice of our arts.

Let us, then, first save ourselves a world of trouble by substituting the notion of untranslatability for that of absoluteness. In this way we shall learn better than to expect serious light upon music from the acknowledged external subjects of the 'Eroica' and 'Pastoral' Symphonies. On the contrary, it will be our knowledge of the music that will throw light upon those subjects; and we shall appreciate the full impertinence that would destroy our capacity for listening to music by encouraging us to think of unauthorized subjects which we gratuitously suppose the music to illustrate. I have already pointed out that the word *Bild* is a fairly exact German translation of the Greek word idea', and that it therefore does not authorize us to attach a very pictorial meaning to Beethoven's statement that he always had an idea of what he was writing. This is perhaps not quite a fair translation of what he said, but there can be no dispute about another important statement of his, which is that his themes hardly ever occurred to him as vocal, but always as instrumental, ideas. This qualification at once removes the composer from the circumstances in which musical themes are most likely to be associated with words. Beethoven and Schubert are, in fact, the last of the classical composers to take lessons in vocal declamation as part of an academic course. They both submitted themselves to Salieri, whom there is reason to believe that Beethoven consulted with a deliberate sense that a training in Italian declamation was as necessary to musicians as a training in the sister art of counterpoint. Both arts were in a state of obsolescence, and in both Beethoven felt his natural talent to be inadequate.

Now the art of Italian declamation had a venerable history, at every stage of which musical idioms became symbolically related to words. There was no reason why the musical symbols should not have their own absolute musical beauty, and hence there was no reason why musicians should long remain conscious of the symbolism. Where the composer is thus conscious, the identifying of his musical symbolism may be a matter of high aesthetic importance. This is unquestionably the case with John Sebastian Bach, and the scholarship of Pirro and Schweitzer has been of inestimable value in revealing to us some of Bach's deepest intentions, as well as his more mechanical associations of ideas. It is not more than amusing to trace an automatic reaction that impels him to rise in the scale on mentioning the High Priest. It would be silly for us to imitate such a habit; and it would be pedantic to blame Bach for not troubling to inhibit it. But many radical misinterpretations of Bach's tempi and expression can be prevented by due knowledge that certain types of figure are definitely associated by him with joy, grief, divine wrath, &c. One of the greatest of French organists confessed himself baffled by the abstruse harmonies and textures of Bach's chorale preludes until the young organist Dr. Albert Schweitzer was introduced to him as a student who had made a special study of these compositions, and who pointed out that the explanation of every detail could be found in the words of the hymns. It is, indeed, a fascinating task to trace in any of Bach's chorale preludes the particular verse that he has in mind. The only point in which I find myself respectfully differing from the great French organists is that I have always felt that the French harmonic theorists from Rameau onwards have suffered so much from disciplinarian logic that Bach's harmonic style always transcends their theories, whether it be symbolic or not. My own mind has never been so amenable to such discipline as to demand a verbal explanation for any audacity in Bach's harmonies. Moreover, if any detail in Bach's works failed to satisfy me as music, no amount of verbal symbolism would make it more acceptable to me.

The habits of musical symbolism unquestionably helped Bach to get on with his work, and the study of them unquestionably saves us from many such appalling misconceptions about tempi and expression as are recorded by Czerny as based upon the way in which Beethoven, with no access to Bach's vocal music, played the Forty-Eight Preludes and Fugues. But it has been well said that the function and power of music in relation to words is not to illustrate them, but to *versinnlichen* them, to make them sensuous. The fall of Adam has brought death and destruction into the world. Bach's glorious chromatic harmony is even more powerful than the sound and sense of the opening verse-paragraph of *Paradise Lost* to arouse in us the sense of repentance and conviction of sin, and it is a mere confusion of thought that sees anything quaint in the fact that Bach's pedal-bass seems to give a literal meaning to the word 'fall' by its appearance on paper. Such accidental quaintness is enhanced by the juxtaposition of this chorale with another on the text *Erstanden ist der heil'ge Christ*, where the pedal-bass illustrates the word 'arisen' in the same kind of way.

In Proske's *Musica Divina* we may amuse ourselves by accusing Marenzio and Victoria for having divergent views about the behaviour of the saints in glory, who, clad in white robes, follow the Lamb whithersoever It goeth, for, while both composers agree to set the word *sequuntur* in imitative scales, Victoria makes the scales descend and Marenzio makes them rise. But it is quite clear that neither composer would feel comfortable in representing the word *sequuntur* by canon in contrary motion, and it ought to be equally clear that they achieve a much nearer approach to absolute music by yielding to their habits of musical symbolism than they could ever hope to attain by resisting them. It is obvious that, even if music were to remain so inveterately descriptive of other things, this kind of verbal symbolism could contribute very little to its meaning.

The poets themselves have always known this far better than the modern musical supporters of descriptive declamation. As I have already pointed out, Wagner himself makes Hans Sachs say that the tune of Walther's prize-song is lovely to write poetry to; and Mendelssohn once had the patience to answer what might have been a tiresome inquirer with a very profound piece of philosophy, explaining that the meaning of his *Songs Without Words* was far more definite and far more likely to be the same for all persons than any words—that, for instance, to some persons the words 'Praise the Lord' might convey the same kind of cheerfulness which the notion of a day's royal sport might convey to another; so that Mendelssohn's understanding of the words would depend upon his knowledge of the speaker, whereas a piece of music would convey its meaning the more unambiguously for being untranslatable. Several editions of Mendelssohn's *Songs Without Words* have been published with unauthorized titles. Most that I have seen are stupid and commonplace, though none has approached the perversity of a series of poems, of which a friend has told me, in which each song without words has been set with serious intention to sentiments consistently opposite to anything the music can convey to musical people. For instance, the poet appears to have heard nothing in the C minor Song except the rhythm of its accompaniment, which he interprets as a trot. The steadiness and energy of the rhythm undoubtedly give strength and a certain expression of courage to the melancholy melody that lies above; but it does not justify the poet in assigning that melody to 'merry Hussars'. The poet should have handed his task to Queen Victoria, whose criticism of an alleged drinking-song was that 'you couldn't drink a cup of tea to that'.

The absoluteness of music is forced upon musicians by every unauthorized attempt to fit music to the purpose of other arts. Brahms's Fourth Symphony, for instance, has been used as music for a ballet. The third and fourth movements of the symphony might seem to invite such a proceeding, inasmuch as Brahms confessed that the third movement was first inspired by the sight of a famous frieze representing a procession of Bacchanals, and the finale is in the tempo and form of a passacaglia, which is originally a dance-form; but even in these movements the emotional and dramatic contents are such as cannot but be weakened by association with the most sublime of ballets. And the rest of the symphony is about as amenable to expression in ballet as the whole drama of *Hamlet* or *King Lear*. The failure to appreciate the enormous concentration and intensity of absolute music is not surprising when we consider that the historic origins of absolute music arise from dance and from the singing of words. Moreover, the teaching of composition is incomparably more practical if it takes account of these origins than if it ignores them or tries to exclude them. From the middle of the nineteenth century onwards academic musicians made the fatal mistake of confusing between the accomplished absoluteness of music and the means of attaining it. The editors of the first standard editions of the complete works of

Mozart and Beethoven descended to the imbecility of publishing full scores of operas without the spoken dialogue. This faulty abstraction of the music from its surroundings extended, and in some places still extends, to the practice of opera-houses, in which the conductor of the orchestra was completely out of touch with the stage-manager, and the stage-manager might almost have been selected for his ignorance of music. Wagner rendered that state of things obsolete, but musicians proceeded to retard matters by dividing themselves into absolute musicians and Wagnerians. Mozart is now recognized as the unique miracle of a composer who was supreme both in opera and in instrumental music; but for practical purposes he is like the giraffe : there ain't no such animal.

Perhaps the work that has done most to preserve music from drying up on one side into false abstraction and spreading into a dismal swamp of omnium gatherum on the other side is Beethoven's glorious failure in opera. Any child can see that *Fidelio* is all wrong, but, as a recent critic has well remarked, it nevertheless makes most other operas seem shabby. Sir Henry Hadow put his finger on the spot that is nearly fatal to *Fidelio* as an opera, but he drew the wrong inference from it. There are defects in the libretto, and in the handling of the necessary conventions of its operatic forms, which make the work unconvincing as a drama, though its story is thrilling enough in as far as we can understand it. Hence *Fidelio* contains many passages which its defenders will describe as unmistakably dramatic. 'Yes,' said Sir Henry Hadow, 'but only as the D minor Sonata is dramatic.' It is surprising that a critic not only so eminent as a writer, but so excellent as a musician, should allow himself to imply that a sonata is less dramatic than an opera. The dramatic events of a sonata move ten times as fast as any stage drama; and no stage music could support five minutes of music at the normal emotional concentration of the sonata style. The stage is the region of art in which a very little goes a long way. The most elaborate stage machinery produces its greatest effects with colours splashed by the pailful on to wooden boards. Staginess seen by daylight in the open air is not more glaring nor more gorgeous than a framed easel-picture. It is flimsy, dingy, and rough. One of my most amusing experiences was that of being haunted by the memory of a mighty climax which I could not place in any Wagner opera, though I could conceive of no drama less emotional than *Tristan* which it could fit. The difficulty in finding a place for it in Wagner was that I knew that it subsided into a delightful kind of moonlit coolness far less tropical than any Wagnerian climate, even in *Die Meistersinger*. I eventually ran it to earth, or rather to heaven, in the coda of a movement by Brahms which most people would describe as of statuesque dignity. There is no drama and no epic that can achieve the intensity of absolute music.

The artist who commands the expressive powers of the classical symphony and the string quartet must learn not so much to restrain them as to dilute them almost beyond all recognition when he brings his music into relation with stage drama. There is at present a fashionable wave of anti-Wagnerianism among our musical aesthetes. The critical sensations which it expresses are merely the normal disillusions that arise when we see stage scenery spread on the ground in the open air by daylight. You can reproduce these disillusions on any scale and in any art by viewing large-scale objects through a magnifying glass: as you can by placing one of Beethoven's long preparatory passages against a background of Mozart, by setting one of Mozart's wittiest rondo themes against the richer wit and polyphony of a Bach gavotte, and by contrasting the concrete and solid harmonic style of Bach with the ethereal spirituality of Palestrina. In every one of these examples the later style can be made to sound so like an appalling impurity on the background of the earlier that our impression will not be noticeably changed if we substitute bad composers for good ones. Hence we have the deplorable spectacle of our new anti-Wagnerians proclaiming from the housetops their inability to distinguish Wagner from Meyerbeer. It is now almost a generation since this kind of critic was as proudly incapable of distinguishing Meyerbeer from Beethoven, but that state of criticism is now definitely dated as Edwardian. Fashion is recovering some common sense in regard to Wagner, whose popularity rests, indeed, on foundations so broad, as well as so deep, that even the protests of sensitive artists like Debussy are recognized by the general run of opera-goers as merely the cries of overstrained nerves, excusable when emitted by a composer whose own original output justifies its existence. All artists with strongly marked styles of their own may be excused if they tend to judge the works of other artists as things they would or would not have cared to write themselves. Sometimes it is easiest to be generous towards things you would never have cared to write.

In any case, artists are much better occupied in getting on with their own work than in trying to put their criticism of other artists on a correct metaphysical basis. The enjoyment of absolute music should be the goal of every music-lover. I have needed more than three and a half lectures to illustrate how this enjoyment is delayed by the fact that music has been compelled to develop through combination with all manner of extra-musical things. The most illustrative music, sung with words and accompanied with dramatic action, must in the last resort justify its existence on absolute musical grounds. Hence, I consider myself to have been already speaking of absolute music throughout this whole course of lectures. On the other hand, the purest of absolute music will remain true to the rhetorical principles which the art has learnt from its association with the human voice; and of all impurities that can vitiate music I am not sure that the generalized abstract form imposed upon it from without is not the worst.

The true art-forms of absolute music are the most powerful means of artistic expression within my experience. I do not know any climaxes or cumulative effects in other arts that can compare with a great return to the home tonic, a great cumulative coda, or a great break into a new movement. One contrast in *Paradise Lost* does, indeed, happen to impress me as something to which I can find no adequate musical parallel, and that is the effect of the passage beginning 'Hail, holy Light', which bursts upon us after we have been with the fallen angels in darkness, and have followed Satan in his escape towards what we expect as daylight, but find ourselves in the full light of Heaven itself. Though music may not have anything as sublime as this, the poet cannot impart to it anything like the immediate shock of a musical contrast. In the long run I find myself more deeply impressed by the substance of Milton's contrast than by that which in some ways resembles it, Beethoven's outburst into the finale of the C minor Symphony; but the whole C minor Symphony covers not merely a Miltonic, but a Shakespearian, dramatic range in half an hour. Milton's one contrast needs four books of poetry to give it its proper effect, and I must distribute the reading of *Paradise Lost* over several days before I can have any impression of it as a whole at all. The persons who can achieve and retain a unified musical impression of an epic poem must be few and gifted with much more vivid memories than that of the average musician, who is often perfectly capable of knowing a work like the C minor Symphony by heart, and who is in far greater danger of becoming callous to his classics than any lover of literature.

The experienced musician who has taken proper care of his musical digestion will not become callous; and we musicians cannot fail to be struck by the inadequacy of the notions of absolute music current among other artists. Far be it from me to attempt quantitative or qualitative comparisons between different arts. Even in comparing one work of art with another there is the fallacy inherent in all attempts at arithmetical operations upon infinite quantities. There are different orders of infinity, which we may call higher and lower, in as far as they exist in finite numbers of dimensions. And a work of art acquires the quality of infinity as soon as it has perfectly digested its materials: a consummation by no means impossible, because, as the diminutive duellist said when he proposed to chalk an outline of his size upon the body of his gigantic adversary, 'anything outside will not count.'

So far as I know, Sir Henry Hadow is the first writer on music who has made a weighty statement about the intense depth and power of absolute music. The support of an authority so eminent on all questions of educational values gives me my only hope that non-musicians may come to recognize something independent of professional pride in my protest against the inadequacy of current musical estimates. I have already grumbled at the habit of poets to recognize nothing in music between the dying of soft voices and the trumpet's loud clangour. No poet has spoken adequately of music since Milton, whose father was not less competent as a musician than as a scrivener. Browning is not a very convincing exception. He took a positive pleasure in choosing the wrong names for his musicians. Master Hugues exists only to rhyme with fugues, Abt Vogler was a real person, but an appalling humbug, and Stanford has cruelly pointed out that the chromatic decline of Vogler's sublime musical edifice, with its 'gliding by semitones and blunting into a ninth', &c., has an unfortunate resemblance to the trailer forced upon the average organist by the slowness with which the clergy and choir settle down. Nevertheless,

Browning has a great and noble idea of music, though he allows himself to accept gross misinformation about it such as would never have deceived Milton. The most crass academic blundering of the day is revealed when Browning says: 'Schumann's self was no worse contrapuntist'. Schumann is a composer whose resemblances to Browning include a genius for experimenting in art-forms closely parallel to those of Browning's dramatic lyrics and a robust friendliness which encourages sentimental people to wallow in his ruminations with an easy conscience; but Schumann, though unorthodox, was definitely a great contrapuntist, whose counterpoint was as smooth as Browning's diction was rough.

The non-musician's failure to measure the importance of absolute music has no doubt been largely caused by the range of the external subjects which composers have identified with their programme music. Beethoven's own verbal explanations of his music should always be suspected as if they were traced to poor Schindler. Other and more serious explanations by composers themselves will often give a wrong impression, simply because the composer is trying to explain an art which he has thoroughly mastered in terms of another art which he has not mastered at all.

Even if the composer is as great a master of literature as Schumann, Berlioz, and Dame Ethel Smyth, difficulties will always arise from the fact that the literary explanation will not be directed to the same recipients as the music, for no musician can wish words to intrude between him and another musician. All musicians feel towards verbal explanations as a man of science feels towards popular exposition. It may be excellent practice; and the ripeness of a scientific theory may be measured by its capacity for popular explanation—not, perhaps, without an uneasy suspicion that that capacity is a symptom of over-ripeness.

To an absolute musician the art of opera, unless grossly misunderstood, reveals more of the nature of absolute music than the wisest verbal criticism. The whole sum of Beethoven's musical experience before he wrote *Fidelio* had far less effect than that single work in deepening and intensifying his later style. The literary value of classical opera-libretti is notoriously too slight to support any statement about the scope of music; and, apart from ritual and the Bible, the association of great music with great literature is extremely rare and has achieved harmony only on a small scale: the scale, let us say, of Parry and Milton, *At a Solemn Music*, and of Brahms's *Gesang der Parzen*. Gounod's *Faust* is a very successful opera, and even Ambroise Thomas's *Hamlet* holds the stage; but the listener with any literary sense can tolerate the libretti of these works only by reducing all thought of Shakespeare and Goethe to the level at which parody is amusing, while only the fear of being thought priggish can induce a serious musician to more than a toleration of Gounod's vulgarity for the sake of the occasional spontaneous aptness which that vulgarity has not inhibited. No adequate music has yet been written for *Faust*; and even for Goethe the subject of Faust became a melting-pot into which Goethe poured anything and everything that occurred to him and to the world in his later years.

The later style of Beethoven has been compared with the second part of *Faust*, but the comparison, though in many respects brilliant, ultimately expresses little more than a feeling that both are sublime and that both contain elements of conflict not only unsolved but insoluble. But I have never been able to find any insoluble conflict within the elements of Beethoven's later style. There is, indeed, an insoluble conflict between his later forms and the forms laid down in text-books, but that sort of conflict did not take place in his own mind, and ought never to have happened at all. His fugues are notoriously his harshest compositions; and their harshness so often coincides with a conspicuous scholastic device that nothing is easier than to accuse him of an anxiety to propitiate academic critics by such things. The accusation is as childish as the weakness it imputes. Beethoven's fugues are at an emotional and dramatic tension which can propitiate nothing. Their devices are identifiable with all manner of scholastic forms. These forms can be shown to be adapted to Beethoven's dramatic purposes by means that did not exist in fugue music until Beethoven applied them. We can describe these means in words, and must so describe them if we are to point them out at all; but we need not suppose that Beethoven arrived at them in so ridiculously roundabout a way as to lay down a verbal description for a rule and then follow it.

In *Die Meistersinger*, when Hans Sachs has given the justly exasperated Walther a long and poetical apology for the existence of rules in master-songs, Walther, who has that night dreamt the substance of his prize-song, asks: 'How am I to learn the rules?'

To which Hans Sachs answers: 'Lay them down yourself and follow them. Think of this morning's dream, and leave the rest to Hans Sachs.' Poetry, as I have remarked before, cannot digest a metaphysically correct theory of art; and Sachs's words have to my knowledge misled musicians into laying down for themselves *a priori* rules which, being based on mere revolt from experience, are far sillier than any that have been codified by academicians: such a rule as, for instance, that whole movements of chamber music should be written without rests for any of the instruments. What Hans Sachs ought to have said was: 'Let your dream lay down the rules, without prejudice to its power to alter them; see that nothing but your dream shall alter them; and then obey it implicitly.'

Some of the anti-Wagnerians of the present day are very great musicians, but not great in a way that gives their judgement the authority of a free mind unpreoccupied with its own work. Wagner had no means of understanding Brahms; the Brahminen, from whom we should exempt Brahms himself, had no means of understanding Wagner; and the anti-Wagnerians of the present day have so many and such various ways of misunderstanding music that I can see nothing in common with them except a tendency to discover the fundamental working hypothesis of one art-form after another, and to describe that hypothesis as a fatal defect. It is this state of things that makes me conceive the project of analysing Wagner's *Ring* as a piece of absolute music. Of course, such an analysis will not proceed very far before it will suggest to any experienced musician that Beethoven's C sharp minor Quartet concentrates into fifty perfect minutes incomparably more music than all that Wagner expresses in four days. But we ought to have known that before we attempted to analyse any music at all. I am quite confident that a purely musical analysis of Wagner's *Ring* will reveal a marvellously consistent style and a musical form, the perfections of which are immeasurably more important than its most obvious defects. To compare it with a Beethoven string quartet would be as silly as to inspect stage-scenery by daylight with an eye still focused on the details of an easel-picture. But it would be equally idle to deny that on the Wagnerian scale ideas are expressible which are entirely beyond Beethoven's scope—not beyond his scope in sublimity or depth, and not beyond his powers of suggestion; but facts are facts, and dimensions are very important facts. Macaulay illustrated a profound aesthetic truth when, remarking that size was an important element in architecture, he instanced the Great Pyramid and asked what could be more vile than a pyramid thirty feet high. Many popular concert-room extracts from Wagner, such as, for instance, the *Walkürenritt*, are in the miserable condition of a pyramid thirty feet high. You cannot handle time as if it were space. I take a string quartet of Beethoven rather than a symphony as an illustration of absolute music at its greatest, not because the Ninth Symphony appears to descend from the summit of its absoluteness to a choral finale, but because the time-dimension is the same for the quartet as for the symphony, and the C sharp minor Quartet covers the widest emotional and musical range of anything that I know. Comparison of great works of art are futile, because they are comparisons between infinities.

The fallacies that are prevalent concerning absolute music are mainly the fallacies of regarding musical forms as abstract generalities instead of as the natural and inseparable consequences of musical matter however occasioned. I have indicated my reasons for believing that the emotional and intellectual contents of great absolute music are far greater than is implied by anything that has yet been written on the subject, whether in reference to itself or in illustrations from other arts. Logically, I am therefore now obliged to lecture to you in further detail on the greatness of absolute music. This, however, is *ex hypothesi* not expressible in words. I therefore beg you to excuse me from the task of deliberately and of set purpose talking absolute nonsense.

PRINTED IN
GREAT BRITAIN
BY
JARROLD AND SONS, LTD.
THE EMPIRE PRESS
NORWICH